CliffsNotes™

Lipsyte's
The Contender

By Stanley P. Baldwin, M.A.

IN THIS BOOK

- Learn about the Life and Background of the Author

- Preview an Introduction to the Novel

- Explore themes, character development, and recurring images in the Critical Commentaries

- Examine in-depth Character Analyses

- Acquire an understanding of the novel with Critical Essays

- Reinforce what you learn with CliffsNotes Review

- Find additional information to further your study in the Cliffs-Notes Resource Center and online at www.cliffsnotes.com

IDG Books Worldwide, Inc.
An International Data Group Company
Foster City, CA • Chicago, IL • Indianapolis, IN • New York, NY

About the Author

Stanley P. Baldwin received his M.A. in English from the University of Kentucky. He is a writer and teacher living in Nebraska.

Publisher's Acknowledgments

Editorial

Project Editor: Elizabeth Netedu Kuball

Acquisitions Editor: Gregory W. Tubach

Glossary Editors: The editors and staff of Webster's New World Dictionary

Editorial Assistant: Michelle Hacker

Production

Indexer: York Production Services

Proofreader: York Production Services

IDG Books Indianapolis Production Department

CliffsNotes™ Lipsyte's *The Contender*

Published by

IDG Books Worldwide, Inc.

An International Data Group Company

919 E. Hillsdale Blvd.

Suite 400

Foster City, CA 94404

Note: If you purchased this book without a cover, you should be aware that this book is stolen property. It was reported as "unsold and destroyed" to the publisher, and neither the author nor the publisher has received any payment for this "stripped book."

www.idgbooks.com (IDG Books Worldwide Web site)

www.cliffsnotes.com (CliffsNotes Web site)

Copyright © 2000 IDG Books Worldwide, Inc. All rights reserved. No part of this book, including interior design, cover design, and icons, may be reproduced or transmitted in any form, by any means (electronic, photocopying, recording, or otherwise) without the prior written permission of the publisher.

ISBN: 0-7645-8553-3

Printed in the United States of America

10 9 8 7 6 5 4 3 2 1

1O/RY/QV/QQ/IN

Distributed in the United States by IDG Books Worldwide, Inc.

Library of Congress Cataloging-in-Publication Data

Baldwin, Stanley P.

CliffsNotes Lipsyte's The Contender / by Stanley P. Baldwin.

p.   cm.

Includes index.

ISBN 0-7645-8553-3 (alk. paper)

1. Lipsyte, Robert. The Contender--Examinations--Study Guides 2, Afro-American men in literature. 3. Boxing in Literature. I. Title: The Contender. II Title.

PS3562.I64 C6633 2000

813'.54--dc21

00–038863

CIP

Distributed by CDG Books Canada Inc. for Canada; by Transworld Publishers Limited in the United Kingdom; by IDG Norge Books for Norway; by IDG Sweden Books for Sweden; by IDG Books Australia Publishing Corporation Pty. Ltd. for Australia and New Zealand; by TransQuest Publishers Pte Ltd. for Singapore, Malaysia, Thailand, Indonesia, and Hong Kong; by Gotop Information Inc. for Taiwan; by ICG Muse, Inc. for Japan; by Intersoft for South Africa; by Eyrolles for France; by International Thomson Publishing for Germany, Austria and Switzerland; by Distribuidora Cuspide for Argentina; by LR International for Brazil; by Galileo Libros for Chile; by Ediciones ZETA S.C.R. Ltda. for Peru; by WS Computer Publishing Corporation, Inc., for the Philippines; by Contemporanea de Ediciones for Venezuela; by Express Computer Distributors for the Caribbean and West Indies; by Micronesia Media Distributor, Inc. for Micronesia; by Chips Computadoras S.A. de C.V. for Mexico; by Editorial Norma de Panama S.A. for Panama; by American Bookshops for Finland.

For general information on IDG Books Worldwide's books in the U.S., please call our Consumer Customer Service department at **800-762-2974**. For reseller information, including discounts and premium sales, please call our Reseller Customer Service department at **800-434-3422**.

For information on where to purchase IDG Books Worldwide's books outside the U.S., please contact our International Sales department at **317-596-5530** or fax **317-572-4002**.

For consumer information on foreign language translations, please contact our Customer Service department at **1-800-434-3422**, fax 317-572-4002, or e-mail rights@idgbooks.com.

For information on licensing foreign or domestic rights, please phone **+1-650-653-7098**.

For sales inquiries and special prices for bulk quantities, please contact our Order Services department at **800-434-3422** or write to the address above.

For information on using IDG Books Worldwide's books in the classroom or for ordering examination copies, please contact our Educational Sales department at **800-434-2086** or fax 317-572-4005.

For press review copies, author interviews, or other publicity information, please contact our Public Relations department at **650-653-7000** or fax **650-653-7500**.

For authorization to photocopy items for corporate, personal, or educational use, please contact Copyright Clearance Center, 222 Rosewood Drive, Danvers, MA 01923, or fax **978-750-4470**.

LIMIT OF LIABILITY/DISCLAIMER OF WARRANTY: THE PUBLISHER AND AUTHOR HAVE USED THEIR BEST EFFORTS IN PREPARING THIS BOOK. THE PUBLISHER AND AUTHOR MAKE NO REPRESENTATIONS OR WARRANTIES WITH RESPECT TO THE ACCURACY OR COMPLETENESS OF THE CONTENTS OF THIS BOOK AND SPECIFICALLY DISCLAIM ANY IMPLIED WARRANTIES OF MERCHANTABILITY OR FITNESS FOR A PARTICULAR PURPOSE. THERE ARE NO WARRANTIES WHICH EXTEND BEYOND THE DESCRIPTIONS CONTAINED IN THIS PARAGRAPH. NO WARRANTY MAY BE CREATED OR EXTENDED BY SALES REPRESENTATIVES OR WRITTEN SALES MATERIALS. THE ACCURACY AND COMPLETENESS OF THE INFORMATION PROVIDED HEREIN AND THE OPINIONS STATED HEREIN ARE NOT GUARANTEED OR WARRANTED TO PRODUCE ANY PARTICULAR RESULTS, AND THE ADVICE AND STRATEGIES CONTAINED HEREIN MAY NOT BE SUITABLE FOR EVERY INDIVIDUAL. NEITHER THE PUBLISHER NOR AUTHOR SHALL BE LIABLE FOR ANY LOSS OF PROFIT OR ANY OTHER COMMERCIAL DAMAGES, INCLUDING BUT NOT LIMITED TO SPECIAL, INCIDENTAL, CONSEQUENTIAL, OR OTHER DAMAGES.

Trademarks: Cliffs, CliffsNotes, and all related logos and trade dress are registered trademarks or trademarks of IDG Books Worldwide, Inc. in the United States and other countries. All other brand names and product names used in this book are trade names, service marks, trademarks, or registered trademarks of their respective owners. IDG Books Worldwide, Inc. is not associated with any product or vendor mentioned in this book.

is a registered trademark under exclusive license to IDG Books Worldwide, Inc. from International Data Group, Inc.

Table of Contents

How to Use This Book

CliffsNotes Lipsyte's *The Contender* supplements the original work, giving you background information about the author, an introduction to the novel, a graphical character map, critical commentaries, expanded glossaries, and a comprehensive index. CliffsNotes Review tests your comprehension of the original text and reinforces learning with questions and answers, practice projects, and more. For further information on Robert Lipsyte and *The Contender*, check out the CliffsNotes Resource Center.

CliffsNotes provides the following icons to highlight essential elements of particular interest:

Reveals the underlying themes in the work.

Helps you to more easily relate to or discover the depth of a character.

Uncovers elements such as setting, atmosphere, mystery, passion, violence, irony, symbolism, tragedy, foreshadowing, and satire.

Enables you to appreciate the nuances of words and phrases.

Don't Miss Our Web Site

Discover classic literature as well as modern-day treasures by visiting the CliffsNotes Web site at www.cliffsnotes.com. You can obtain a quick download of a CliffsNotes title, purchase a title in print form, browse our catalog, or view online samples.

You'll also find interactive tools that are fun and informative, links to interesting Web sites, tips, articles, and additional resources to help you, not only for literature, but for test prep, finance, careers, computers, and the Internet, too. See you at www.cliffsnotes.com!

LIFE AND BACKGROUND OF THE AUTHOR

Personal Background

Robert Michael Lipsyte was born January 16, 1938, in New York, New York, the son of Sidney I. and Fanny Lipsyte. He grew up in Rego Park, a neighborhood in Queens. Lipsyte's father was a school principal, his mother a teacher. Young Robert devoted his childhood to books rather than sports. Instead of sharing a game of catch with his father, the two often visited the library.

In the first chapter of his 1975 book *SportsWorld,* which considers the role of sports in American culture, Lipsyte points out that he did not even attend his first major league baseball game until he was thirteen years old, despite the fact that there were three major league teams in New York: the Yankees, the Giants, and the Dodgers. Lipsyte says he was "profoundly disappointed" with the experience and went to only one more game "as a paying customer." His third major league game was as a sports reporter for the *New York Times.*

As a boy, Lipsyte did play Chinese handball against the sides of brick buildings and participated in street games such as stickball, but he felt pressured by society to be good at sports. This experience later developed into a major theme in some of Lipsyte's nonfiction works such as *SportsWorld* and novels like *Jock and Jill* (1982) and his trilogy beginning with *One Fat Summer* (1977). The protagonist of *One Fat Summer*, Bobby Marks, is similar to Lipsyte: Bobby is an adolescent in the 1950s, suffering from a weight problem, who does something about it. In 1952, Lipsyte took a summer job as a lawn boy and lost forty pounds, ridding himself of at least one youthful stigma; Bobby Marks has a similar experience.

Education and Early Work

A Ford Foundation program allowed Lipsyte to skip his senior year at Forest Hills High School in Queens and enroll at Columbia University, from which he earned a Bachelor of Arts degree in 1957 at the age of nineteen. In 1959, Lipsyte received a Master's degree from the Columbia University School of Journalism.

Although he planned to move to California after graduating from Columbia as a nineteen-year-old English major, Lipsyte took a summer job as a copy boy in the sports department of the *New York Times.* Eventually becoming a sports reporter and then a sports columnist, he stayed with the newspaper for fourteen years. During that time, he co-authored *Nigger* (1964) with controversial comic and activist Dick Gregory; published *The Masculine Mystique* (1966); wrote his first and best-known novel, *The Contender* (1967); and published an edited collection of his columns, *Assignment: Sports* (1970).

After 1971, Lipsyte worked as a freelance writer, television scriptwriter, journalism professor, radio commentator (National Public Radio, 1976–82), and columnist for the *New York Post* (1977). He was a television sports essayist for *CBS Sunday Morning* (1982) and stayed with that network until moving to NBC in 1986. After leaving NBC in 1988, he hosted *The Eleventh Hour* on PBS (1989), winning an Emmy Award for On-Camera Achievement although the show was canceled after its second season. Returning to the *New York Times* to write a sports column in 1991, Lipsyte continued freelance writing while beginning a column in 1992 in the magazine *American Health.*

Lipsyte married Maria Glaser in 1959; they divorced in 1963. In 1966, he married novelist Marjorie Rubin; they had a son, Sam (1968) and a daughter, Susannah (1971). His second marriage ended in 1987. He married television producer Katherine L. Sulkes in 1992.

Career Highlights

Lipsyte's novels for young adults have gained considerable critical acclaim for their absence of sentimentality as well as for the excellence of his writing. Lipsyte's characters do not necessarily win an ultimate prize at the end of the novel. They are more likely to go through an admirable change due to effort and personal growth.

Lipsyte has written two sequels to *The Contender.* In *The Brave* (1991), protagonist Sonny Bear is a seventeen-year-old half-Indian runaway who meets Alfred Brooks, now a forty-year-old policeman, in New York. Alfred rescues Sonny from a drug war and teaches him to box. In *The Chief* (1993), Sonny tries to become a heavyweight champion and must deal with problems similar to those that Lipsyte learned about as a sports journalist.

Some of the most successful of Lipsyte's works, other than *The Contender* (1967), are those in the trilogy featuring Bobby Marks: *One Fat Summer* (1977), *Summer Rules* (1981), and *The Summerboy* (1982). All take place in Rumson Lake, an upstate New York resort town. Bobby deals with problems like those that other young adults might face between the ages of fourteen and eighteen. In the first novel, he is known as the "Crisco Kid" because of his obesity. He must deal with a local bully named Willie Rumson who enjoys humiliating Bobby. In addition to losing weight, Bobby learns to stand up for himself. In the second novel, Bobby is sixteen and faces a more complicated dilemma. His old enemy, Willie Rumson, is falsely accused of arson. Bobby knows that his girlfriend's troubled younger cousin set the fire, and he must decide whether to tell the truth. Bobby is eighteen in the third book and dealing with unsafe working conditions at a laundry where he is employed. Speaking up will likely lose him his job.

Works of Nonfiction

Much of Lipsyte's nonfiction deals with sports, but here again he rarely takes a conventional approach. He is especially concerned that children are subjected to sports in negative ways. Sports should be fun and entertaining; winning need not be the only goal. Although he is not anti-sport, he is disillusioned by a culture of champions that he calls "Sportsworld." SportsWorld, as Lipsyte points out in the book by that name, "is a grotesque distortion of sports." It honors the winner more than the race. As illustrated in *The Contender*, Lipsyte values the process more than the result; competing well is more important than winning itself.

Lipsyte was among the first to accept and respect the unconventional prizefighter Muhammad Ali. His agreement that Ali should be allowed to be himself is echoed in the title of his 1978 book on the complicated man: *Free to Be Muhammad Ali*.

In 1978, Robert Lipsyte was diagnosed with testicular cancer. Despite his eventual recovery from that first bout, he was diagnosed with cancer a second time in 1991. His experience with the illness led to another novel for young adults, *The Chemo Kid* (1992). In it, the protagonist, Fred Bauer, an ordinary high school junior in almost every way, discovers he has cancer and undergoes a series of experimental hormone treatments. Miraculously, Fred acquires superpowers, apparently due to the treatments, and becomes "The Chemo Kid," fighting for the environment and against drug dealers.

An adult consideration of cancer, and sickness in general, is Lipsyte's 1998 nonfiction work, *In the Country of Illness*. Here, he speaks of infirmity as if it is a foreign land, a place he calls "Malady . . . another country, scary and strange." Basing his accounts on his own experiences, as well as those of other family members, he comforts, advises, warns, and informs the reader with tenderness, insight, and wit. Lipsyte's second wife, Margie, learned that she had breast cancer after their divorce. Especially moving is the account of Lipsyte's second wife Margie's failing health, after being diagnosed with breast cancer, and the strength shown by Margie and their two young adult children.

In addition to the Emmy, Lipsyte's honors and awards include the Dutton Best Sports Stories Award, E. P. Dutton, 1964, 1965, 1967, 1971, and 1976; the Mike Berger Award, Columbia University Graduate School of Journalism, 1966 and 1996; Wel-Met Children's Book Award, 1967; *New York Times* outstanding children's book of the year citation, 1977; American Library Association best young adult book citation, 1977; and New Jersey Author citation, 1978.

INTRODUCTION TO THE NOVEL

Introduction

In his excellent critical biography, *Presenting Robert Lipsyte*, Michael Cart repeats Lipsyte's account of how the sports journalist first got his idea for *The Contender*. Lipsyte was in Las Vegas to cover a heavyweight championship fight between Muhammad Ali and Floyd Patterson, scheduled for November 22, 1965. The night before the fight, he had a conversation with legendary boxing manager Cus D'Amato, then in his late fifties. D'Amato reminisced about the days when he worked in his gym on New York's Lower East Side. As with Donatelli's Gym in the novel, a prospect had to climb three flights to present himself. D'Amato had a special interest in the kids who, like Alfred, came running up the stairs afraid and alone. He compared that fear to fire, which can "burn you or keep you warm; it can destroy you or make you a hero, a contender in the ring and in life." The metaphor inspired Lipsyte. In his own life, he says, "becoming a contender meant writing a novel."

A Brief History of Harlem

To get the most out of reading *The Contender*, the student should have some understanding of the historical and cultural context in which the story takes place. History and culture are one in the Harlem of the 1960s, and some knowledge of that setting helps in appreciating Alfred and his world.

In 1658, a Dutch governor named Peter Stuyvesant named a village on northern Manhattan Island "Nieuw Haarlem" after Haarlem in the Netherlands. Africans, slaves of the Dutch West India Company, built the first road into the area in the seventeenth century. African American slaves worked the land for Dutch and, later, English farmers for nearly 200 years. In 1790, one third of the area's population was made up of slaves. The village developed as a fashionable white suburb of New York City in the 1800s. Real estate prices soared but later collapsed due to excessive speculation in the early 1900s. The Lenox Avenue subway line connected Harlem with lower Manhattan at about the same time, and blacks began moving in. By 1930, the African American population of Harlem had soared to 180,000.

Black Harlem in the 1920s and 1930s was a cultural Mecca, home to the center of an intellectual and cultural movement known as the Harlem Renaissance. As Jim Mendelsohn points out in an essay for

Africana.com, many of the residents were reasonably well off financially, in neighborhoods like Stridel's Row on West 139th Street. They supported churches such as The African Methodist Episcopal Zion and newspapers such as the *Messenger*. W. E. B. Du Bois, a founder (in 1910) of the National Association for the Advancement of Colored People (NAACP), edited the organization's magazine, *Crisis*, along with Jessie Fauset.

Social life and the arts flourished, sometimes together, as the Lincoln and Apollo theaters, the Cotton Club, and the Savoy Ballroom provided first-class entertainment. Paul Robeson was known worldwide for his singing and acting as well as his controversial politics. Tap dancer Bill "Bojangles" Robinson was called "The King of Harlem." Writers such as Langston Hughes, artists such as Jacob Lawrence, and musicians such as Fats Waller and Duke Ellington contributed to the explosion of creativity.

However, many blacks were struggling even in the 1920s, and whites owned most of the businesses. The Great Depression, beginning in 1929, hit hardest the poor. Employment improved during the United States' involvement in World War II (1941–45), but Harlem's economy sank in the next twenty years. By the 1960s, when *The Contender* takes place, housing conditions had deteriorated; there were extensive slums. The African American middle class, made up of people like the novel's Aunt Dorothy and Uncle Wilson, left Harlem for suburban areas like Queens. The repressive mood of Lipsyte's first chapter is justified. It is the Harlem that Alfred first wants to escape and then wants to change.

Black Nationalism

The "nationalist rally," which Alfred and his family pass on their way to church at the beginning of Chapter 4, and whose supporters Alfred later encounters, further reflects the culture of the time. During the century from the Civil War (1861–65) to the setting of the novel (1960s), African Americans struggled with the question of whether to try to live with whites or separate from them. Marcus Garvey, who founded the Universal Negro Improvement Association in 1916, led one of the first popular black nationalist movements. However, it was Elijah Muhammad's Nation of Islam (NOI) and Malcolm X's Organization of Afro-American Unity (OAAU) that dominated the black nationalist scene in Harlem in the 1960s.

The roots of the NOI were in Detroit, where a salesman named Wallace D. Fard (pronounced fa-ROOD) founded the Temple of Islam in the early 1930s. In just a few years, Fard developed the Temple into a force for economic independence and racial separatism. He advocated the rejection of white society and warned against the evils of the "blue-eyed devil." Fard taught strict adherence to religious principles through his University of Islam and the Muslim Girls Training Corps. White authorities came to distrust Fard as a violent subversive. Fard disappeared in 1934 when he was offered a choice of leaving Detroit or going to prison. Elijah Muhammad, Fard's top lieutenant, took charge of the Temple of Islam and was the most powerful black nationalist in the country for the next forty years.

Elijah Muhammad moved the NOI's headquarters to Chicago where he built the Temple of Islam Number 2 in the latter 1930s. Under Muhammad's leadership, there were eventually more than one hundred temples nationwide. He further emphasized financial growth for the NOI, sometimes drawing criticism for the Nation's leaders' accumulation of worldly possessions. The disciplined lifestyle of the black Muslims made them attractive employees, and the workers donated freely to the NOI.

The NOI glorified women but severely limited their freedom. Their role was domestic and parental, and their purity was to be above reproach. However, critics pointed out that NOI leaders sometimes used women as sex objects; Elijah Muhammad himself allegedly fathered several illegitimate children.

The NOI flourished in the late 1950s and 1960s even as it stood in contrast to the Civil Rights Movement, which was led by Dr. Martin Luther King, Jr., and sought peaceful integration. During this period, one of the NOI's most charismatic leaders was Malcolm X, head of the Harlem Mosque; he was a former prison inmate and brilliant speaker who was especially effective in large groups and on television. One of his catch phrases was that the movement should fight white racism and violence "by any means necessary." Despite the popularity of Malcolm X, the NOI censured him in 1963 for his notorious remark that the assassination of President John F. Kennedy was tantamount to "the chickens coming home to roost." Malcolm X left the NOI in 1964 and formed the OAAU. Many blamed the NOI when he was assassinated the next year.

The question of race was complicated in Harlem in the 1960s, and Lipsyte does not dodge the issue. Certainly we see the results of white racism against blacks in *The Contender.* But in the first chapter of the novel, we also see Major and his gang using racial slurs in an attempt to intimidate and manipulate Alfred. Even more blatant is their prejudice against Jews. Consistent with racial stereotypes, they accuse the Jewish grocers of indulging in greed ("They go pray for more dollars") and a modern form of slavery, exploiting black employees for mercenary purposes. When Alfred tries to defend the Epsteins, he only causes more problems. Major and his undisciplined gang would be a disgrace to the NOI, but many of the racial issues are the same.

A Brief Synopsis

The Contender is a coming-of-age novel whose protagonist, a black seventeen-year-old high school dropout named Alfred Brooks, lives with his Aunt Pearl and her three daughters in Harlem, a predominantly African American neighborhood in Manhattan, New York City, in the mid-1960s. Alfred's father deserted the family when Alfred was ten years old; his mother died when he was thirteen. On both occasions, his best friend, James, stood by him.

Now, Alfred and James seem headed in opposite directions. One Friday night in June, James breaks into Epsteins' grocery with members of a street gang led by the novel's antagonist, a bully named Major. Alfred is a clerk at the store and inadvertently reveals that there may be money in the cash register on a Friday night; he forgets to tell James about the new alarm system recently installed. Only James is arrested; he is put on probation. Meanwhile, Alfred begins training at Mr. Donatelli's Gym. A wise mentor, Donatelli insists that no one is promised anything, everyone is treated equally, and a man finishes what he begins. The journey, the climb, is more important to Donatelli than the highest goal. Striving is key. Alfred should try to become a *contender* and let the championships of life come if they will, according to Donatelli.

Alfred begins training at the gym and progresses well. As a spectator, he attends a fight night at Madison Square Garden. When challenged later that evening, he is able to stand up to Major, leader of the street gang. However, Alfred's training is long and sometimes tedious. Alfred cannot yet trust himself; he is too susceptible to the opinions of others. Alfred's employers, the Epsteins, seem to doubt him after the burglary. Eventually, Alfred weakens. He attends a party at the gang's clubroom, indulges in alcohol and marijuana, and passes out. Alfred sees James at the clubroom and discovers that he has become addicted to heroin. Both boys seem lost.

After a hellish Sunday at Coney Island with Major and the gang, Alfred decides to quit boxing. When he visits the gym to clean out his locker, he finds Mr. Donatelli alone. In attempting to apologize to his mentor, Alfred finds that he does not really want to quit. He needs to find out what he could become if he really tries. He reaches a sort of epiphany, a moment of clarity and self-awareness. He wants to become a *contender*.

Alfred resumes training with renewed enthusiasm. Soon, he is allowed to spar, and in October he has his first amateur fight at a union hall on Long Island. Alfred makes rookie mistakes but wins. Especially impressive that night is an older welterweight named Elston Hubbard. In November, Alfred knocks out his second opponent but is terribly upset because he thinks he has nearly killed the other fighter. His third fight, in December, is a draw, because Alfred is reluctant to throw a punch. Mr. Donatelli advises him that it is time to quit. Alfred lacks the "killer instinct" necessary to go very far, and he could be seriously injured in the ring. Alfred has one more fight scheduled, and he insists on finishing what he has started.

Just before fight time, Alfred, a lightweight, learns that his final opponent is Elston Hubbard, the older, bigger, and stronger ex-Marine who fought so well the night of Alfred's first fight. Donatelli wants to cancel, but Alfred knows he must go on. He barely survives the first two rounds and is dominated by Hubbard. Nevertheless, Alfred finds a few tactics that work, and the third round is a war. Standing toe-to-toe in a brutal exchange, Alfred refuses to fall. He goes the distance. Although he loses a unanimous decision, Alfred knows that he has won the important fight. He has proven to himself that he can persevere and be a contender in life, as well as in the boxing ring.

But Alfred has one more task to accomplish. James is in deep trouble. Apparently stoned, he crashed through the front window of Epsteins' grocery in an awkward attempt at burglary. Alfred finds him at a secret cave where the two hung out as boys. Applying his new attitude and some tough love, Alfred convinces James that there is hope; he helps James to the hospital.

With the encouragement of his college-educated cousin, Jeff, and a schoolteacher called "Spoon," who used to be a fighter, Alfred will finish high school and work with young people in public recreation. He has become a true *contender*.

List of Characters

Alfred Brooks The protagonist of the novel, Alfred hopes to transcend the repressive atmosphere of Harlem and find a worthwhile life for himself.

James Mosely Alfred's best friend, James descends into drug addiction as Alfred climbs toward maturity.

Aunt Pearl Conway James' mother's sister. Pearl provides a home and spiritual base for Alfred; she works as a domestic for a white family, the Elversens.

Charlene, Sandra, and Paula Aunt Pearl's giggly daughters provide a family for Alfred.

Aunt Dorothy and Uncle Wilson Pearl's sister and her husband. Their family lives in the suburbs and provides Alfred with a look at a very different kind of life.

Cousin Jeff Aunt Dorothy and Uncle Wilson's college-educated son, who brings significant encouragement and friendship to Alfred near the novel's end.

Diane Jeff's younger sister; a cousin and friend to Pearl's daughters.

Major The primary antagonist of the novel, Major leads the gang and confronts Alfred until the protagonist sees him for the bully and coward that Major is.

Hollis, Sonny, and Justin As gang members, they are subservient to Major.

Mr. (Vito) Donatelli Owner and head manager at the gym, he serves as Alfred's mentor.

Clarence "Bud" Martin Donatelli's top assistant, he supports and critiques Alfred.

Henry Johnson Disabled by a childhood bout with polio, Henry is a rising apprentice trainer with special devotion to Alfred.

Bill "Spoon" Witherspoon A former fighter who has become a schoolteacher, Spoon serves as exemplar while he encourages Alfred to finish his education.

Betty Witherspoon Bill's wife is also a teacher. She dislikes boxing but cheerfully helps Alfred prepare for his fights.

Dr. Corey A dentist whose office is in the same building as the gym, Dr. Corey makes Alfred's first mouthpiece, a significant rite of passage for the aspiring boxer.

Jelly Belly The rotund Jelly's real name is Horace Marshall Davenport, Jr. Jelly Belly provides comic relief and occasionally wise observations.

Red A bad example of attitude, he picks a fight with the elder but shrewder Bud Martin at Donatelli's Gym.

Angel and Jose The lighthearted Puerto Rican fighters are friends of and valuable sparring partners for Alfred.

Willie Streeter One of Donatelli's most promising fighters, he is an example of wasted potential as he loses to Junius Becker, fails to train properly, and drops out of sight.

Elston Hubbard Easily the best of Alfred's opponents, Hubbard dominates the first two rounds but gets all he can handle from Alfred in the third.

Lou, Jake, and Ben Epstein The brothers own the grocery where Alfred works as a clerk; Lou was once a fighter known as "Lightning Lou Epp" and is especially concerned about Alfred.

Harold and Lynn These young black nationalists attempt to recruit Alfred and suggest that he help with recreation programs for black children in the community.

Reverend Price and Sister Lucille The storefront preacher and his wife put on a lively Sunday service; he later convinces Aunt Pearl to allow Alfred to pursue boxing.

Character Map

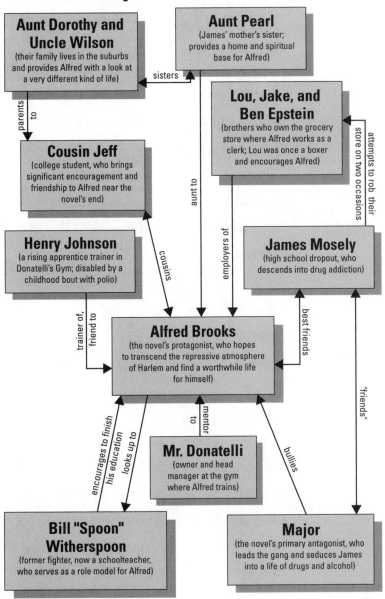

Aunt Dorothy and Uncle Wilson
(their family lives in the suburbs and provides Alfred with a look at a very different kind of life)

Aunt Pearl
(James' mother's sister; provides a home and spiritual base for Alfred)

sisters

Lou, Jake, and Ben Epstein
(brothers who own the grocery store where Alfred works as a clerk; Lou was once a boxer and encourages Alfred)

parents to

Cousin Jeff
(college student, who brings significant encouragement and friendship to Alfred near the novel's end)

attempts to rob their store on two occasions

aunt to

Henry Johnson
(a rising apprentice trainer in Donatelli's Gym; disabled by a childhood bout with polio)

cousins

employers of

James Mosely
(high school dropout, who descends into drug addiction)

trainer of, friend to

Alfred Brooks
(the novel's protagonist, who hopes to transcend the repressive atmosphere of Harlem and find a worthwhile life for himself)

best friends

"friends"

encourages to finish his education

looks up to

mentor to

bullies

Bill "Spoon" Witherspoon
(former fighter, now a schoolteacher, who serves as a role model for Alfred)

Mr. Donatelli
(owner and head manager at the gym where Alfred trains)

Major
(the novel's primary antagonist, who leads the gang and seduces James into a life of drugs and alcohol)

CRITICAL COMMENTARIES

Chapter 1

Summary

The setting is Harlem, a black neighborhood in the northeast corner of Manhattan in New York City. The time is the mid-1960s. It is twilight on a Friday. As the novel opens, Alfred Brooks, an African American seventeen-year-old high-school dropout, waits on his apartment building's front stoop for his best friend, James. When Alfred was ten years old, his father left home; when he was thirteen, his mother died of pneumonia. On both occasions, Alfred's pal James stood by him. Now, Alfred lives with his Aunt Pearl and her three young daughters, Charlene, Sandra, and Paula.

James is late, and Alfred suspects a problem. Alfred believes his friend may be in bad company. Alfred hurries to the basement clubroom where he finds James with Major, Hollis, and Sonny. While Alfred tries to persuade James to go to the movies with him as they had planned, Alfred inadvertently reveals that his employers, the Epsteins, leave money in the cash register of their grocery store on Friday nights so that they don't handle money on the Jewish Sabbath. Major, who has been mocking Alfred for his subservient duties at the Jewish store, quickly sees an opportunity for easy cash. Major leads Hollis, Sonny, and James on a raid of the grocery; Alfred refuses to go along.

After the others have left, Alfred suddenly remembers that the Epsteins have installed a new silent burglar alarm. He tries, too late, to warn James. Several police cruisers descend on the grocery. Hoping that James has escaped, Alfred searches for him at their secret cave in the park.

Later, Hollis, Sonny, and Major blame Alfred for James' capture. The three attack Alfred, but he escapes a savage beating when two policemen appear in the distance, scaring off the gang members.

Commentary

The first chapter is rich with symbolic imagery. Ragged, skinny children play with empty beer cans. Police sirens fill the night and remind

Alfred of Harlem's despair and the conflict with authority. Yet there are lovers in the park, music, and dreams.

Literary Device

The setting is crucial to the novel. In this opening chapter, Lipsyte provides his first descriptions of Alfred's Harlem. As Lipsyte presents it, the atmosphere of Harlem is repressive. The sun, often a literary symbol of hope and promise, melts into the hopelessness of "the dirty gray Harlem sky." Even the air is rancid and foul; Lipsyte describes it as "sour air." Men drag card tables out onto the sidewalks, and we can imagine the shrill sound of table legs scraping across concrete. Lipsyte's description recalls the sound of cars crunching through garbage and broken glass. These sounds underscore the overall feeling of the backdrop that Lipsyte is painting. He wants us to *hear* those sounds; he wants us to *see* the gray sky; he wants us to *smell* the sour air. Lipsyte wants us to feel the grit of the neighborhood and to recreate this atmosphere in our imaginations.

Two dominating images introduced in this chapter are the clubhouse and the cave. The clubhouse is a shabby basement room with a naked light bulb. Major dominates it with his mocking pessimism. It is a home for lost souls who are going nowhere, and Alfred regrets that James chooses to spend his time there. When the two were younger, they shared their fantasies and ambitions in the secret cave. James enthusiastically collected rocks, planning to exhibit them at school in the fall. However, when he took them home from the cave, his drunken father dumped them down the air shaft. In fact, most of James' dreams have been destroyed in a similar way, symbolically.

In this chapter, Lipsyte effectively combines dramatic action with exposition. He introduces the reader to major themes of the novel, key characters, and images that will recur and come to symbolize important contrasts in Alfred's life.

Theme

The major themes of *The Contender* center around Alfred's growth from a somewhat lost high school dropout to a young man with discipline and realistic goals. This is a story of choices. In this chapter, Lipsyte portrays Alfred choosing to resist peer pressure and refusing to participate in the burglary of his employer's grocery.

Theme

Another major theme of the novel is the contrast between hope and despair. Despite his father's abandonment and his mother's death, Alfred finds a source of hope in Aunt Pearl's loving wisdom. Although he has dropped out of school, Alfred has not yet surrendered to the sense of loss that surrounds him; his friend James apparently has.

Several key characters, introduced by Lipsyte in this chapter, immediately align themselves with major themes in the novel. Alfred is the *protagonist*, the main character around whom the action centers. Confused though he may be, Alfred is making an effort to be responsible and to help support his household. He works as a stock boy at a grocery store and gives most of his pay to his Aunt Pearl. He refuses to accept Major's stereotypical mocking of the Jewish employers. Alfred seeks escape and hope through his private dreams, once shared with James in the privacy of their secret cave and now renewed on Friday nights at the movies.

Major is the *antagonist*, the main opponent of Alfred. Major's power is wholly negative. He enjoys his role as bully and viciously teases Alfred for trying to succeed. James is caught between Alfred and Major, and he is rapidly losing hope in his future.

A brief appearance by the physically disabled Henry, who loves boxing, foreshadows a crucial change in Alfred's life. Henry invites Alfred to Donatelli's Gym. Aunt Pearl, who also appears only in passing, is a stabilizing force who provides Alfred with at least some guidance, something he will need more of during the course of the novel.

Glossary

(Here and in the following chapters, difficult words and phrases, as well as allusions and historical references, are explained.)

Harlem section of New York City, in northern Manhattan; it borders on the Harlem River channel and the East River; here, the area traditionally inhabited by African Americans in the 1900s.

Old Uncle Alfred Major contemptuously implies that Alfred is an "Uncle Tom" [Informal], a black whose behavior toward whites is regarded as fawning or servile. The term refers to the main character, an elderly black slave, in Harriet Beecher Stowe's antislavery novel, *Uncle Tom's Cabin* (1852).

synagogue a building or place used by Jews for worship and religious study. Here, it relates to the Jewish Sabbath, which runs from sundown Friday to sundown Saturday and is observed by the Epsteins, the owners of the grocery store where Alfred works.

squeeze the eagle to be stingy; a reference to the insignia of the eagle on U.S. currency. Here, it implies that the Jewish grocers are reluctant to let go of their money, a racist stereotype.

skull caps light, closefiting, brimless caps, usually worn indoors. Here, the reference is to yarmulkes, which are worn by Jewish men in (and sometimes outside of) synagogue as a sign of respect for God.

The Man [slang] here, a reference to authority, specifically to white authority and the police, even though some policemen in the novel are black.

Chapter 2

Summary

James is in jail. Alfred awakes in Aunt Pearl's apartment and learns from Aunt Pearl that Henry Johnson found Alfred wandering around the previous night, beaten but not permanently injured, and that Henry and Henry's father carried him home. When Aunt Pearl asks how he was hurt, Alfred tells her that he fell off a fence, but she doesn't believe him. After Aunt Pearl goes to work and his cousins go out to play, Alfred tries to eat a little and watches some television (where he sees a show depicting a white suburban family, whose life stands in stark contrast to his own); but he spends most of the day asleep.

That night, Alfred goes out, avoiding streets where he might meet Major or his henchmen. Alfred sees Henry Johnson but avoids him, too, because he is in no mood to express gratitude. Without consciously meaning to, Alfred winds up in front of the building housing Donatelli's Gym. Alfred thinks he spots Major in the distance and runs across the street, but he realizes that the man he saw is not his adversary, and he feels ashamed. He wonders if he will always be a slave to fear. Although Alfred shakes with uncertainty, he somehow climbs the stairs to the third-floor gym where he meets a stocky, stoic older man. Alfred says that he has come to be a fighter.

Commentary

Literary
Device

In this chapter, Lipsyte makes especially effective use of setting. Aunt Pearl's apartment is a haven for Alfred. He is tempted to stay there and sleep indefinitely. Through the window, he hears the some-times sweet, sometimes threatening street sounds of Harlem: children playing, horns honking, a quartet of street singers' blending harmony, a police siren forcing reality through the joy. The street is especially dangerous for Alfred this night. As he leaves the building, a little boy on the stoop tells him that Major and Sonny are hunting for him. For reasons that even Alfred does not understand, he arrives at Donatelli's Gym, which recalls Henry's invitation to Alfred in the first chapter to join him at the gym, as well as Alfred's apparent contempt for the gym and Henry's mundane job there.

Literary Device

The gym, too, is a kind of haven; but unlike the cave and the apartment, it is a haven that must be *earned*. Lipsyte's imagery is often specific and strong, but never more so than in Alfred's original ascent to Donatelli's Gym. Symbolically and literally, Alfred has to climb to get there. The stairs represent a psychological and spiritual climb even more than a physical one. A quivering chill runs up Alfred's legs; his teeth grind; a ball of ice forms in his gut. The staircase reeks of "stale wine and antiseptic and sweat and urine and liniment." Hundreds of steps seem to loom before him. This is more than just a staircase, and Alfred knows it.

Glossary

Lenox Lenox Avenue in Harlem.

big cats here, other African American men.

spoons and needles paraphernalia used in the preparation of drugs, specifically heroin.

Joe Louis African American boxer Joseph Louis Barrow (1914–81), world heavyweight boxing champion (1937–49). Louis was revered by blacks for his leadership, athletic prowess, and demeanor.

Sugar Ray Robinson African American boxer; original name, Walker Smith (1921–89); outstanding boxer, world welterweight and five-time middleweight champion.

Chapter 3

Summary

Donatelli is a stocky man with crew-cut white hair. He carries himself in a military manner and is very businesslike, even brusque, as he first measures Alfred (five feet seven and three-quarter inches tall) and then weighs (124 ½ pounds). Donatelli tells Alfred exactly what to expect if he tries to become a fighter. He invites the young man to return but suggests that he not do so unless Alfred is genuinely prepared to commit himself to the program.

Commentary

Theme

Lipsyte uses this chapter for transition (presenting a major change in Alfred's life) and to introduce a key character, Donatelli, as well as the new boxing regimen that Alfred is about to begin. The wise old manager offers several guidelines to Alfred, and each is a theme of the novel as well as a lesson in growing up. In a boxing ring, just as in life, there is no place to hide. Alfred must learn to follow the rules. He must earn his way. Skill is essential and can be learned, but skill is not enough. Nothing is guaranteed. If Alfred quits before he really tries, he has failed more than if he had never started at all.

Style & Language

Most importantly, as the title of the novel indicates, Alfred must strive to be a *contender* rather than a champion. The chances are that Alfred will never reach the top, but he will be a contender if he takes his skill, his brain, and his heart as high as he can. "That must sound corny to you," Donatelli tells Alfred, and it does seem like a cliché; but what Lipsyte and Donatelli understand is that a cliché often becomes a cliché because it carries a deep truth.

Style & Language

This chapter is a transitional one, but it is almost a dramatic monologue as well, serving as one of many examples of the way that Lipsyte uses speech to reveal character. Throughout most of the book, the dialogue is reasonably realistic. As a reporter and sportswriter, Lipsyte is familiar with the sounds of Harlem and of boxing in the 1960s.

Perhaps he cleans up the language a bit; but when Major speaks in the first chapter, we get a good idea of the kind of person he is. When Major mocks Alfred as an Uncle Tom, the language evokes a strong visual image. With different effect, the same is true in Chapter 3. There is no jive in Donatelli, but his speech reveals as much about his character as Major's speech does about his. Donatelli's speech is as straight as his posture and contrasts noticeably with Major's. The challenge to Alfred is clear. What Alfred does in response to the challenge will determine the action of the rest of the novel and, ultimately, the direction of his life.

Glossary

duffel bag a large, cylindrical cloth bag, especially of waterproof canvas or duck, for carrying clothing and personal belongings.

Chapter 4

Summary

It is Sunday morning. Alfred accompanies his three little cousins and Aunt Pearl as they walk to church. The five pass a rally featuring a street speaker who advocates racial separation and resistance to white control. As Major did in the clubroom in the first chapter, the speaker taunts Alfred for trying to fit into the white man's world. Alfred recognizes Harold, a stocky, politically oriented young man whom he knew in high school. Harold and a slender young woman named Lynn try to recruit Alfred, but he hurries on to church.

After worship services, Alfred, Aunt Pearl, and the girls ride the subway to Jamaica, a suburban village in Queens, to visit Pearl's sister Dorothy and her family. Dorothy's husband, Wilson, has a good job and has purchased a house. Their son, Jeff, has a scholarship to college and may join the Peace Corps. At the end of the day, Alfred, Aunt Pearl, and the girls return to Harlem. After Aunt Pearl and the girls fall asleep, Alfred takes Aunt Pearl's alarm clock from her room and sets it for 5:30 a.m.

Commentary

Literary
Device

This chapter presents sharp contrasts. The serenity and cheer of Aunt Pearl and her brood clash with the anger of the nationalist rally. Lipsyte presents two public speakers early in the chapter. The first is the shaven-skulled man on a stepladder who stirs up the street crowd. He says that the "white man's got his foot on your throat" and encourages violence when he asks if the blacks intend to continue to turn the other cheek. Easily spotting Alfred as a churchgoer, he accuses him of worshipping the white man's God. He calls Alfred a "Tom." Soon after, Harold calls Alfred "a happy little darky." Reverend Price, in contrast, preaches a Christian message of tolerance and cooperation. He warns against agents of the devil who advocate hatred of the white man.

The settings in this chapter also contrast sharply. Lipsyte describes Jamaica as a tranquil little village with grassy streets and tidy houses. Aunt Dorothy and Uncle Wilson are clearly well off financially. They live the black suburban dream. On the subway back to Harlem, Alfred worries about a large black man, drunk and bleeding in the middle of the subway car. In Harlem, the streets seem dirtier, the apartment smaller.

Alfred is very aware of this disparity. Even his cousin Jeff contrasts with Alfred in a disturbing way. Jeff is held up as an example, a huge success. He won all the prizes at high school graduation and earned a scholarship to college. Jeff was president of his sophomore class and may join the Peace Corps after graduating from college. He plans to work in a voter registration school in the South this summer. Alfred, meanwhile, faces a Monday morning with cans to stack and floors to sweep at the grocery.

Still, Donatelli's message has stuck, echoing in his head: "Nothing's promised you. You have to start by wanting to be a contender." Alfred sets his alarm for 5:30 in the morning, foreshadowing his decision to become a contender.

Glossary

nationalist rally Here, the term suggests the black nationalist movements of the 1960s, specifically the Nation of Islam, led by Elijah Muhammad (1897–1975), and the Organization of Afro-American Unity (OAAU), founded by Muhammad's former protégé, Malcolm X (1925–65).

Tom [Informal] Uncle Tom; here, another stereotypically derogatory reference to the main character of *Uncle Tom's Cabin*.

Peace Corps an agency of the United States, established in 1961 to provide volunteers skilled in teaching, construction, etc., to assist people of underdeveloped areas abroad; here, the agency Alfred's cousin Jeff may join after graduating from college.

Queens the largest borough of New York City, on western Long Island, east of Brooklyn; the home of Alfred's Aunt Dorothy and Uncle Wilson.

Chapter 5

Summary

Alfred is running in the park at first light Monday morning. His stride is smooth and easy. Birds sing, the breeze is cool, and he feels a rare joy. Alfred Brooks is smiling.

Suddenly his reverie is smashed by two policemen, one of whom shouts, "Hold it right there." Alfred explains that he is in training, managed by Mr. Donatelli. The cops have heard of Donatelli and ease off. The mood, however, is broken. The good feeling is gone. When Alfred returns home, Aunt Pearl also wonders why he was out at such an hour, but Alfred tells her that he couldn't sleep and went for a walk.

At work, Lou Epstein, the oldest of the brothers, speaks privately with Alfred about the burglary. He says that Alfred is "a good boy," but the employers seem distant and distrustful. Jake, the middle brother, takes the deposit to the bank; this had been Alfred's job. Surprisingly, James, his face swollen and grim, appears at the window as Alfred is arranging fruit in the front window. He doesn't respond to Alfred's greeting. Alfred is despondent and fantasizes about robbing the store himself. Suddenly Henry pops in, oozing energy. He is delighted that Alfred will be at the gym after work. Before Alfred can refuse, Henry is gone.

Commentary

Character Insight

Alfred's hold on his new life is tenuous. He wavers between hope and despair. In this chapter, we see a young man at a crossroads in life, and he is struggling to determine which path to take. One continuing problem for Alfred is that he can be excessively influenced by those around him. (This will be a more serious problem for Alfred later.) He is just beginning to be his own man, another theme of the novel. Lipsyte demonstrates Alfred's vulnerability in three very different settings in this chapter.

Alfred's first challenge is in the park. He is trying a new regimen, and at first everything goes well. He is up at 5:30 a.m. and soon on the run. Sweet air fills his lungs. Although he is just beginning to get in shape, and a sharp pain runs through his side, Alfred is filled with joy. A silly smile crosses his face. He is a healthy young man who feels the gratification of accomplishing something. Still, this sense of self-worth is so fragile that it can be (and is) destroyed by a single exchange with the two policemen. Even though they quickly believe Alfred and laughingly wish him well, Alfred's run is ruined. The spring leaves his step. The stitch in his side is now unbearable. He notices gas fumes from cars. Soon he quits and goes home.

At the apartment, even Aunt Pearl questions his odd behavior. She asks if he has been out all night. In her loving way, she expresses her concern for Alfred's safety. As he often does, Alfred evades the truth. Instead of providing a candid response, he says he was out for a walk. He is not yet able to be a man and take responsibility for his choices, even when they are admirable. Alfred is still afraid to be himself.

At work, Alfred's day gets even worse. The Epsteins say they have faith in him, but their actions say otherwise. For Alfred's own sake, Lou Epstein says, it may be better not to present Alfred with too much temptation. Alfred is crushed when he sees that this means he will no longer be trusted with the bank deposit. James also rejects him, turning away from Alfred when he sees James standing outside of the grocery; James walks away like Major. Alfred feels like giving up and notices a way to disengage the new alarm system. Maybe he could regain James' friendship if the two of them robbed the store.

Alfred's problem is that he has not yet learned to believe in himself. If he did, it would matter less what others think. Alfred wants to escape to the safe, dark dream world of the movie theater. However, Henry's grinning intervention reminds him of the scheduled gym workout. Through it all, Alfred salvages enough hope to give the new life another try.

Glossary

sneakers shoes with a canvas upper and a continuous sole and heel as of one piece of soft rubber, used for play and sports; the shoes worn by Alfred on his morning run.

welfare the organized efforts of government agencies that grant aid to the poor, the unemployed, etc.; such aid. Here, the term relates to Aunt Pearl's reminders to Alfred that the family is not on welfare, that they have jobs and enough money to pay the rent and buy clothes.

probation the suspension of sentence of a person convicted but not imprisoned, on condition of continued good behavior and regular reporting to a probation officer; here, James' punishment for attempting to rob Epstein's grocery store.

bunions places on the foot showing an inflammation and swelling of the bursa at the base of the big toe, with a thickening of the skin. Here, the term refers to Lou Epstein's bunions.

Chapter 6

Summary

Alfred retrieves the euphoria of his morning run as he bounces up the "friendly" stairs leading to Donatelli's Gym. He tries to stifle his grin before entering, because he wants to look businesslike and tough when he greets the manager for his first day of training. But when he opens the door this time, he is greeted not by Donatelli but by a sight that reminds him of Reverend Price's description of hell.

The gym appears to be in chaos. Young men of several races and all sizes are participating in activities completely foreign to Alfred. Some perform gyrations that resemble jacks-in-the-box. Others seem to be boxing their own images in mirrors. A very rotund person flies past, spraying him with sweat "like a lawn sprinkler." Alfred is totally unprepared. He doesn't even have proper gear and must work out in his street clothes. Donatelli is absent, preparing a fighter for an appearance at Madison Square Garden that night. Dr. Corey, the dentist from the second floor of the building, finally greets him in a friendly manner. Still, most of the crowd ignores him. An arrogant, well-built fighter called "Red" treats him rudely. Red is eventually expelled by Bud Martin, Mr. Donatelli's cagey old assistant.

Commentary

Theme

Chapter 6 introduces Alfred, and the reader, to the world of Donatelli's Gym. Despite the apparent disorder, the gym runs by a strict system of honesty and effort. Within the confines of the gym, Donatelli and Bud Martin set and enforce the code. It is a way of life that a young person like Alfred might apply very effectively to the outside world. Individuals are responsible for their own behavior. They must earn everything they get. It is, consequently, a *meritocracy*. Individuals will receive only what they merit or deserve.

Literary
Device

Lipsyte uses the character Red as a literary device to illustrate the code by opposing it. Red wants to be treated like his idea of a champion, but he has done nothing to earn it. When Red demands that someone tape his hands, Bud Martin tells him to learn to do it himself. When Red tries to get Henry to fetch a headgear for him so that he can spar, Bud Martin rescinds the order and reminds Red that he can spar only if Mr. Donatelli or Bud can monitor the activity. Donatelli is gone, and Bud is busy. Bud tells Red that he needs to learn to follow the rules. Red challenges Bud just as he challenges the system. He even tries to punch the old man in the mouth, but the wily Bud knows how to defend himself. He knocks Red's punch aside and raps the misfit in the jaw with his own stinging blow. Red is kicked out, but Bud reminds everyone that no one needs to mention the incident to Mr. Donatelli, because another part of the code is that everyone gets a second chance.

Several minor characters contribute to the atmosphere, some of whom appear later in the novel. Denny is a skinny white boy who is friendly to Alfred and teaches him to do sit-ups in the manner that was acceptable at the time. Two Puerto Rican boxers impress Alfred with their quickness and skill. Jelly Belly is the enormous black man who inadvertently sprays Alfred with sweat and is a supporter of the system.

Initially, Alfred feels alone and like an outsider when he enters the gym, but he goes ahead anyway. When he is alone on the mat doing sit-ups and pushups, he doesn't want Henry to walk away. But Alfred overcomes that feeling of loneliness again. Bud Martin has a final surprise for Alfred. Donatelli has left a ticket with Henry so that Alfred can attend the evening match at the Garden. Alfred's will to overcome his fears is paying off.

By the end of the chapter, Alfred and the reader have a pretty good idea of the world in which the protagonist will try to become a man. We already suspect that manhood has more to do with character than with physical toughness.

Glossary

jack-in-the-box a box from which a little figure on a spring jumps up when the lid is lifted, used as a toy. Here, the term is used to set the scene in Donatelli's Gym when Alfred first arrives.

medicine balls large, heavy, leather-covered balls, tossed from one person to another for physical exercise.

the Garden Madison Square Garden, a center for sporting activity, especially boxing, in New York City.

spar to box with jabbing or feinting movements, landing few heavy blows, as in exhibition or practice matches.

Cassius Clay Cassius Marcellus Clay, Jr., (1942–) won the light heavyweight championship at the 1960 Olympics. He joined the black Muslims (Nation of Islam) in 1964 and changed his name to Muhammad Ali, winning the world heavyweight championship three times and earning a worldwide reputation for his outspoken opinions on the Vietnam War, the military draft, politics, religion, and race.

Chapter 7

Summary

When Alfred accompanies Henry to that night's fights at the Garden, he enters yet another new world with its attendant revelations on boxing and life. Outside the building is a vast array of fight fans ranging from seedy men with smashed-in faces to high-rolling Harlem gamblers in dinner jackets. Inside is a scene that is both threatening and exciting.

Mr. Donatelli's promising prospect, Willie Streeter, is to meet Junius Becker in the featured event. Alfred is very impressed with Willie, who looks cool and confident. Jelly Belly, who has joined Alfred and Henry, is more skeptical, noting that Willie is Willie and will likely fight the fight "*his* way" despite Mr. Donatelli's instructions. Alfred briefly thinks of James and the fun they once had pretending that they would be professional wrestlers.

The fight is surprisingly slow until the middle rounds when the two combatants inadvertently smash heads. Becker briefly goes to a knee, but it is Willie who has a serious cut on the outside corner of his left eye. Willie seems to quit fighting, and Becker takes the offensive. Donatelli asks the referee to stop the fight, granting Becker a victory. In the locker room, the three friends meet Bill Witherspoon, a former fighter and schoolteacher, who gives Alfred and Henry a ride home. On the stoop of Alfred's building, Major, Hollis, and Sonny are waiting for him.

Commentary

Literary
Device

The opening paragraph of Chapter 7 is an excellent example of Lipsyte's use of dynamic imagery to set the tone and describe a scene. In addition to the variety of people in the crowd of hundreds gathered around the entrance to the Garden, Alfred is intrigued by the mixed smells of perfume, mustard, and beer.

Inside the Garden, Alfred at first feels threatened because everyone seems to be angry. Alfred thinks they are angry with him. As he often does, Lipsyte makes effective use of repetition as the usher scowls, the program seller scowls, the ticket taker scowls, and even the snack stand attendant scowls. Soon, however, Alfred notices that they scowl at everyone.

Character Insight

Donatelli asks the referee to stop the fight not because Willie's cut is so bad but because Willie has stopped fighting. Donatelli realizes that Willie does not have the heart to be a top fighter and will only be injured and embarrassed if the fight goes on, foreshadowing later events in Alfred's coming of age.

In contrast to Willie is Bill Witherspoon, affectionately know as "Spoon." Spoon had been a very good fighter, once rated the "Number Seven light-heavyweight contender." Good as Spoon was, he was getting beaten too hard. Although he was still winning, Mr. Donatelli one day said to him, "Billy, I think it's time." Donatelli urged Spoon to return to college, and Spoon is now "Mr. Witherspoon," a successful teacher. Spoon's experience, too, foreshadows later events in Alfred's journey.

The night has been rewarding for Alfred, and he is in fine spirits as he walks home from Henry's house. Lipsyte, though, is far from ready to let Alfred, or the reader, off the hook.

As Alfred approaches his own front stoop, dreaming of being a champion, Alfred spots three figures standing in wait. They are his adversaries: Hollis, Sonny, and Major.

Glossary

marquee a rooflike structure or awning projecting over an entrance, as to a theater; here, the marquee at Madison Square Garden, advertising the fights.

attaché cases flat, rectangular cases, as for carrying documents; briefcases; here, referring to the cases being carried by businessmen going to the fight.

showed some dog did not give his best effort; a derisive term.

Chapter 8

Summary

Major and his henchmen have taken Alfred to the clubroom where they attempt to intimidate him. They want him to help in another burglary of the Epstein brothers' grocery. Alfred is to do what he earlier considered: disconnect the alarm. Although he literally quakes with fear, Alfred refuses to cooperate. Major attempts to bully him and even pulls a knife, but Alfred holds his ground. Major is the one who buckles. Alfred returns home feeling victorious.

Commentary

As Chapter 8 opens, Alfred has been forced to go to the clubroom with Major, Hollis, and Sonny. This situation could be a very dangerous one for Alfred, recalling the way these three boys seriously roughed him up when they caught him alone at night at the end of Chapter 1. The implication of Alfred's first confrontation with the three boys was that the beating would have been much worse had two policemen not come along.

Now, however, Alfred is able to get Major to back down by standing up to him. Major is a bully and a coward, but a reasonable reader might question whether the outcome is realistic. Major is humiliated in front of his sidekicks and lamely gives Alfred three days "to decide" whether he will help with the burglary even though Alfred repeatedly refuses to do so. The result tells us more about Major than it does about most gang leaders in general. Fortunately for Alfred, Major is bluffing.

Chapter 9

Summary

Although it is only his second day of training, Alfred feels loose and strong on his run the next morning. His life appears to be improving rapidly. Even a policeman yells encouragement. Alfred runs for more than an hour and does calisthenics on his way back to the apartment. At home, Aunt Pearl again questions where he has been and is relieved when Alfred now is able to tell her the truth. She would prefer that he not box, but it is better than what she had imagined he was doing.

Commentary

Character Insight

The significance of Chapter 9 rests in Alfred's change in his response to Aunt Pearl. When she questioned him Monday morning (Chapter 5), he avoided telling her where he has been. On Tuesday morning (Chapter 9), he tells her the truth. Alfred is now proud to be on the road to becoming a boxer. Still, he does not yet grasp Mr. Donatelli's message. He thinks of himself as a would-be *champion*, not a contender. Alfred Brooks shows promise, but he has a long way to go.

Chapter 10

Summary

Over the next few weeks, Alfred experiences the hard work and tedium of training to become a fighter. The first week is mostly pain. Mr. Donatelli has him shadowboxing for three minutes, resting for one minute, and shadowboxing for three minutes again, to the point that Alfred awakens in the middle of the night in misery. The second week is more of the same but worse. Alfred feels that everyone is riding him. At Sunday morning service, Aunt Pearl asks Reverend Price about the boxing. Alfred secretly hopes that the preacher will make him quit, but Reverend Price wisely sees this as a positive way to direct the young man's energy for a while.

Halfway through the third week, the pain subsides. Alfred is getting in shape. He wakes up before the alarm in the morning and runs smoothly. Still, Alfred feels isolated. Spoon drops by and pays some attention to him, but days pass when no one says a word. At work, Lou Epstein reveals that he was once a fighter known as "Lightning Lou Epp." Alfred is impressed. Lou respects Donatelli and Bud Martin but is skeptical about the way that the profession of boxing has changed. He appears to genuinely care for Alfred.

Alfred grows weary of the routine of training. He wants to get in the ring and spar. He is beginning to wonder what the point of it all is. In late July, Aunt Pearl has to go out of town; she leaves the girls in Queens with Dorothy and Wilson, and Alfred has the apartment to himself.

Alfred runs into Major on the street one night, and Major claims that he was just "testing" Alfred that night at the clubroom when Alfred stood up to him. Major tries to get back into Alfred's life. He comes by the gym, but Bud Martin asks him to leave. Major says that James will be at a "little party" at the club that night; he wants Alfred to drop by. Henry is suspicious of Major's motives.

Henry asks him to join Henry and Jelly at the movies that night. He warns against visiting the clubroom. Alfred declines and walks into the hot Friday night, telling Henry that he can take care of himself. Alfred notices other people out for a good time and questions the purpose of all the training he is doing. Alfred misses his best friend, James, and wants to get back together with him. At the end of the chapter, Alfred heads toward the clubhouse for a little visit.

Commentary

In these few weeks, Alfred's attitude slides from euphoria to dejection. He still relies on others to confirm his own worth, and he is terribly impatient—two sure signs of immaturity for Lipsyte. Alfred wants to move along in his training, but the Donatelli code demands that no one is special and each man must earn his own way.

Lipsyte's style captures the tedium of the daily workouts at the gym. He repeatedly quotes the trainers as they demand more and more of Alfred in the boring but necessary exercise of shadowboxing: "Left . . . left . . . snap it out, Alfred, . . . left . . . right . . . right . . . left . . . left-left . . ." Like all beginning boxers, Alfred has trouble holding his arms up and continuously punching, three minutes at a time, over and over.

Lipsyte's imagery is again effective. He uses simile (comparing one thing to another with the use of "like" or "as") to make his point. Angel and Jose, the Puerto Ricans, cackle "like hens" when the medicine ball knocks Alfred over "like a tenpin." As Alfred gets into the routine and begins to get in shape, the days roll off "like perspiration," a very apt simile. The Friday night street scene evokes the provocative mix of excitement, danger, and despair that seems to lure Alfred toward trouble. Children play in the gutter, their playground. Each street corner anticipates action of the night. The sun goes down, and music fills the street from windows. It is too hot to sleep, and why should he sleep anyway? So he can rise before dawn and fill yet another day with tedium? The party at the clubroom is very tempting to Alfred in this atmosphere, and he wants to see James. Most of the temptation, however, comes from within.

Willie Streeter appears again as a negative example. He returns to the gym "sullen and overweight." Willie is what Alfred could become at his worst. Willie has given up. He goes off to training camp in the mountains with Mr. Donatelli to train for a fight out of town, but he loses the fight anyway, primarily, we can assume, because of his bad attitude and lack of commitment.

Of special significance is the return of Major. He buzzes around Alfred like a flea in his ear, whispering temptation. When Alfred meets Major on the street, his adversary is cloying and artificially friendly. Major wants to get past his earlier threats, which turned out to be empty. Major wants to be a part of Alfred's life because he sees that Alfred is going somewhere. But Major doesn't just want to ride along; he wants to derail the train. He knows that the best way to reach Alfred is through James, so he tempts Alfred with an invitation to a party at the clubroom that James will attend. Throughout the novel, Alfred runs into barriers not from the outside world but from Harlem itself. Major wants Alfred to fail so that Alfred will be back on the same level as Major is, maybe even a notch lower. Henry sees Major's hypocrisy and tries to guide Alfred away, but Alfred must make his own decisions, and he is about to make a bad one.

Glossary

shadowboxing sparring with an imaginary opponent, especially in training as a boxer; here, the exercise Donatelli has Alfred do to train, the exercise Alfred tires of and sees no purpose in.

tenpin a specific one of the ten bowling pins. Here, it suggests the way Alfred is knocked over by the medicine ball.

racketeers people who obtain money illegally, as by bootlegging, fraud, or, especially, extortion. Here, Lou Epstein uses the term in reference to the bad people he sees affiliated with boxing.

Chapter 11

Summary

When Alfred arrives at the clubroom, the party is in full swing. James, however, is not there. Major assures Alfred, whom he calls "champ," that James will show up. Sonny also refers to Alfred as "champ." It is not likely that either could grasp Mr. Donatelli's concept of the word *contender*.

Initially, Alfred says that he can stay only a few minutes and is in training. Twice he turns down Major's offers of wine. However, the seduction of the party gets to him. Major's girlfriend, June, introduces Alfred to her cousin Arlene, a black girl with a blond wig, dizzying perfume, and an easy attitude. Alfred is surprised at how comfortably she enters his arms to dance to the low, funky blues. From Major, Alfred eventually accepts half an orange soaked with vodka. Major assures Alfred that it is good for him. The party becomes "a sweet, sticky blur." Arlene encourages Alfred to try marijuana, which he does. The only light in the clubroom burns out. More wine and marijuana come around. Alfred feels like he is in a nice, dark movie.

The next morning, still at the party, Alfred feels sick, halfway between intoxication and a hangover. James finally arrives and appears to have been living the hell of an addict. His face is thin. His eyes are sunken. His suit looks too big for him. He has come for a fix. Alfred tries to apologize for the burglar alarm at the grocer and to remind James of their friendship.

"That was kid stuff," says James. He takes a packet of white powder from Hollis and prepares to have a fix; Alfred wants to stop him but is too stoned himself to speak. Alfred falls to the floor and passes out.

Commentary

Character Insight

Upon his arrival at the party, Alfred tries to convince himself, as much as the revelers, that he is still in training and will only stay a few minutes. But this is a form of self-deception and further evidence of Alfred's immaturity. Alfred is not yet prepared to take responsibility for his own actions. Major seems to have been waiting for him and calls him "my main man." Major's date, June, has a girl lined up for Alfred. Although Arlene is not exactly the kind of young woman Alfred would want to introduce to Aunt Pearl, she will still do very nicely for the night. Alfred turns down the wine bottle twice, but he does not require much persuasion after that.

Theme

Through much of the novel, Alfred seeks escape from reality. With James as his partner, Alfred could dream his way out of Harlem through the stories they created at the cave or those they saw on the screen at the movies. Dreams are not necessarily destructive; every goal begins with a dream. The problem is that those dreams had no relationship to reality, which is Mr. Donatelli's point. He does not want his fighters to indulge in unlikely dreams of championships. For Donatelli, and for Lipsyte, sports are not realistic escapes from poverty. Spoon is a positive example for this reason; he used sports to fulfill another dream: becoming a teacher.

James' attempt to escape reality is the most destructive of all. He has become a junkie, a heroin addict. It is not surprising that Major's gang deals drugs. It is just what we would expect of Major. He loves to manipulate people and hold them down. If he can make a profit from it, all the better.

Literary Device

The party is another escape for Alfred. It is not surprising that he compares it to the moment when the light goes out at the movies. The difference is that he is a living part of this movie, and real things are happening. Alfred supposedly came to the party to talk to James, so that he could apologize, renew the friendship, and help him if necessary. The ultimate irony is that, when Alfred finally finds James and wants to dissuade him from using drugs, Alfred himself is too stoned to speak.

Chapter 12

Summary

Alfred parties all Friday night and well into Saturday. It is now Saturday night. He has somehow made his way back to Aunt Pearl's apartment, where he has passed out on the linoleum kitchen floor in a pool of his own sweat. The aggravating sound of the ringing telephone finally brings him to consciousness. It is Aunt Pearl calling to say that she won't return until Thursday. She wants Alfred to call Dorothy the next morning, before church, to tell her that Pearl will pick up the girls Thursday night. Alfred barely hears her. He stumbles to the living room, where he passes out in front of the television. Later, Alfred passes out in the bathroom and finally ends up on the couch. On Sunday morning, he is sick and can't remember the specifics of Aunt Pearl's message.

Around 8:00 that morning, Major telephones to remind Alfred that they are going to Coney Island in a few minutes. Major arrives in a stolen white Cadillac convertible. Hollis, Sonny, and a younger boy named Justin are with him. Alfred reluctantly joins them, and Major drives, often recklessly, to Coney Island. While double-parked in a crowd in front of a lunch stand, Hollis notices policemen checking for drivers' licenses and registrations. The boys abandon the car and split up, Alfred spraining his ankle in the process.

Having escaped to relative safety, Alfred realizes that he has not eaten since noon Friday, almost two full days ago. He buys spare ribs, buttered corn, and French fries, washing them down quickly with a Pepsi. He remembers but ignores Donatelli's warning against such greasy foods. Soon, Alfred is vomiting over the boardwalk railing and onto himself. Later he rests in an air-conditioned movie theater and manages to keep down two cups of ice cream.

By early evening, Alfred has returned by subway to Harlem. He soaks the ankle but won't try to run the next morning. He isn't going to be a boxer anyway. He goes to work Monday and Tuesday but skips his workouts at the gym.

Tuesday night, while just wandering around Harlem, he finds himself in front of the gym and decides to go in and clean out his locker.

Oddly, he feels tears in his eyes as he stuffs his gear into a paper shop-
ping bag. Mr. Donatelli is in the gym but ignores him. Alfred finally
calls to his mentor, says goodbye, and offers an apology. Donatelli says
there is no need to apologize. Alfred asks if he would have been any
good if he had continued. Donatellis answers that there is no way to
know. Alfred asks if he could have been a contender. Donatelli tells him
that only Alfred could answer that question, in time. Donatelli says that,
as a manager, he would know about Alfred only after he was seriously
hurt in the ring for the first time; but Alfred will know then, too. Lipsyte subtly shifts the verb tense in the conversation. Initially, the tense
is conditional, with words like *would*, indicating that Alfred isn't planning to follow through with boxing. But by the end of the conversation, Alfred and Donatelli speak in future tense—"Will you tell me
then?"—indicating that Alfred will continue training.

Commentary

Chapter 12 is one of the most important in the novel. In it, Alfred
reaches his lowest point but experiences a kind of epiphany, a moment
of clarity or self-awareness. Alfred eventually transcends the crisis that
begins with the party and ends, appropriately, in a conversation with
Mr. Donatelli after Alfred has, once more, climbed those symbolic stairs
to the gym.

Literary Device

Lipsyte is a master of imagery, and the imagery is especially powerful as he describes Alfred's further descent and eventual resurrection.
In the first sentence of the chapter, Lipsyte does not say that the telephone is ringing; instead, he writes, "the rattlesnake was buzzing."
Some annoying, probably dangerous force brings Alfred to consciousness. Instead of simply stating that Alfred feels sick, Lipsyte applies
metaphors from the gym where Alfred has spent so many hours training in recent weeks: Jelly Belly seems to sit on his head; Jose and Angel,
chattering too loudly and in Spanish, seem to jump on his stomach;
Mr. Donatelli shouts at him repeatedly. Finally, Alfred realizes that the
noise is just the telephone ringing.

Style & Language

Alfred's trip to Coney Island with Major and his friends is more
like a descent into hell than a trip to an amusement center. It is hot
and noisy. The streets off the boardwalk are "choked" with young people. The smells of cotton candy, fried chicken, barbecue, and hot dogs,
which we might think of as tantalizing, cause Alfred's stomach to

cramp. Babies cry. Fear of the police results in an escape that is chaotic and causes Alfred injury. First, Major nearly runs over a baby carriage in the crowded street. When everyone abandons the car, Alfred badly sprains his ankle, adding to the torture of his flight. When he finally gets something to eat, he vomits it onto himself as well as over the boardwalk railing. Someone calls him "disgusting," and another person thinks he must be a junkie who can't hold down food. Later, he notices dried vomit on his shoes. People back away from Alfred, repelled by the way he smells.

Through all of this, Alfred is tempted to blame Major. Alfred has always preferred to blame someone else for his own mistakes rather instead of accepting responsibility for himself. Here, though, Lipsyte presents a noteworthy change. Alfred finally is ready to grow up and accept responsibility: "Don't blame him, man, he didn't pour all that stuff into you at the party. You did that," he says to himself. Major did not force him to go along that day. It was Alfred's choice. Alfred realizes that he has no one to blame but himself.

Theme

In Harlem, Alfred notices the absence of purpose in the residents, especially the young men. They are just hanging around, "waiting for something to happen." This registers with Alfred, but we are not yet sure if he understands how close he is to joining those people. Although he goes to work on Monday and Tuesday, Alfred, too, is lost. He walks "aimlessly" for hours around Harlem. Reminiscent of his first visit to Donatelli's Gym, Alfred is not consciously aware that he is going there until he arrives. Tears in his eyes, he cleans out his locker as noisily as he can and slams the door shut, apparently hoping to draw Mr. Donatelli's attention. The old man holds no grudge; he wishes Alfred well. Alfred is the one who prolongs the conversation, not wanting to let go. He wonders if he could have been any good, if he could have been a *contender*. Finally, Alfred is asking the right question. It is a question that only Alfred can answer.

Glossary

Coney Island   beach and amusement park in Brooklyn, New York, on a peninsula, formerly an island, at the southwestern end of Long Island. Here, it is the setting for Alfred's final descent.

Cadillac an expensive, top-of-the line automobile made by General Motors. Here, it is symbolic of the most luxurious or highest quality vehicle, a status symbol for Major among his peers in Harlem.

Hudson River a river rising in the Adirondack Mountains in eastern New York State and running generally south to its mouth at New York City, forming part of the New York-New Jersey boundary toward the end of its run.

boardwalk a walk, often made of wood and elevated, placed along a beach or seafront.

Ferris wheel (after George W. G. Ferris [1859–96], U.S. engineer who constructed the first one for the World's Fair in Chicago in 1893) a large, upright wheel revolving on a fixed axle and having seats hanging between two parallel rims, used as an amusement-park ride.

foxes [Slang] persons, especially women, who are attractive, especially sexually attractive.

Brooklyn a borough of New York city, on western Long Island.

smart meat [Slang] a negative nickname used by Alfred to refer to Mr. Donatelli.

Chapter 13

Summary

Alfred is back in training, with renewed intensity. He makes remarkable progress even though the most praise that he receives from Mr. Donatelli is when the mentor says, "Not bad." Alfred knows that, coming from Donatelli, this is very high praise. Alfred spars with Angel, Denny, and Jose and learns how to defeat each of them. Lou Epstein drops by the gym and exchanges greetings with Bud Martin. Bud mentions recently seeing Kid Ryan, a former fighter who once had a great match with Lou. Ryan is not doing well financially, and Lou gives Bud some money to pass on to Kid Ryan anonymously. As they leave the gym together, Lou offers to teach Alfred how to run the cash register.

Commentary

Lipsyte uses this chapter to chart Alfred's progress, primarily in the ring but also with the Epsteins. Alfred learns by sparring with Angel, Denny, and Jose, each of whom presents a different challenge.

Alfred struggles with Angel's style until he learns to apply Bud Martin's advice. Alfred is only throwing one punch at a time rather than working in combinations, attacking with a series of punches. Angel easily slips the one punch and belts Alfred in the gut. Over a period of weeks, Alfred works on the more complicated technique. In a stunning metaphor, Lipsyte speaks of time as if it were an evolving fighter: "August, gasping for breath, melted into September."

Literary Device

The opponents continue to slip Alfred's single jabs. He has a recurring dream: A fly is sitting on his nose, but when he tries to brush it away, he sees that he has no hands. Eventually, Alfred shocks Angel with a dazzling combination of punches that leave the Puerto Rican fighter reeling against the ropes and bleeding. Alfred has nailed the fly. He is not sure how he did it, but Henry, a student of the game, shows him that Alfred's footwork was the key.

Denny's footwork is heavy, but his hands are quick. Alfred learns to stick and move, hitting the opponent with a quick jab or combination and just as quickly dancing away. At this point, appropriately, Lightning Lou Epstein visits the gym and praises Alfred. Demonstrating the trust of the brothers who run the grocery, Lou offers to teach Alfred how to run the cash register, a step up for him and one that involves handling money, illustrating that Alfred has won the trust and confidence of the Epsteins.

Jose is a puncher. He is slower than Angel or Denny, but he has a bruising straight right with which he punishes Alfred's ribs. It takes Alfred three rounds to learn to drop his left elbow to block the punch, leaving Jose's face unprotected. Jose drops "like a sack of potatoes." Donatelli is watching. He tells Alfred to go downstairs to the dentist's to be fitted for a custom-made mouthpiece, a rite of passage indicating that Alfred is ready for his first match.

Glossary

slipped the jab used a defensive technique in which a boxer moves his head just enough to allow the opponent's leading punch to slip by without contact. (It can best be countered by a combination of punches.)

Chapters 14 and 15

Summary

As usual, Alfred's eyes snap open at 5:30 sharp on the morning of his first fight. However, he will not take his usual run this day. Aunt Pearl wonders if he is sick. Alfred is evasive, because he doesn't want her to worry about the fight and is concerned that she might try to stop him from doing it. He says he has a secret. Aunt Pearl respects that.

Henry comes by at 10:00, and he and Alfred meet Mr. Donatelli for lunch at noon. Alfred and Henry take a taxi to Spoon's apartment where Alfred can rest through the afternoon. They are impressed by Spoon's expansive collection of books. Spoon gets home a little after 3:30; his wife, Betty, arrives shortly thereafter and prepares Alfred's pre-fight meal. Spoon speaks briefly of education and tells Alfred that he could finish high school at night if he wanted to.

Alfred lies down and dozes until Henry awakens him. Donatelli has come to ride with them, in Spoon's car, to the Long Island City Union Hall, a large, shabby building that hosts that night's amateur fight card.

Alfred is matched with another lightweight (about 135 pounds) named Rivera. Following amateur rules, they are scheduled for three 2-minute rounds. Rivera is short, wide, muscular, and relatively immobile. Donatelli advises Alfred to "stick and run," which recalls the tactic Alfred used so effectively against Denny, a similar fighter, in the sparring described in Chapter 13. Unfortunately, Alfred is numb with nervousness as he comes out of his corner and walks into Rivera's opening punch to Alfred's mouth. Nevertheless, Alfred quickly recovers and fights well, hitting and moving, until he listens to the jeering of the crowd, taunting him for his evasive fighting tactics. Alfred stands and fights, playing to Rivera's strength, and ends up on the canvas with the referee counting over him. The bell rings to end the first round as the referee reaches "three."

Through the second and most of the third rounds, Alfred fights intelligently, following Donatelli's advice to "stick and run," despite the boos and insults from the crowd. At the end of the fight, however, Alfred thinks he can move in and fight the weary Rivera at close range.

Although he has some success with this approach, Rivera hits him in the groin with a painful blow at the final bell. Alfred wins the fight, but Donatelli is displeased that Alfred allowed himself to be hit at the end.

Back at the apartment after the fight, Aunt Pearl shows concern over Alfred's injuries but reveals that she, too, had a dream when she was seventeen—to join the chorus at the Apollo Theater—but her mother would not allow it. She doesn't necessarily regret the way her life turned out (she has no idea if anything might have come of the singing opportunity), but she regrets not having the chance to try.

Commentary

Alfred's first fight is nothing glamorous. He doesn't even know who his opponent will be until a few minutes before the contest. As Bud says, "[It] ain't Madison Square Garden." In the Donatelli code, however, every fight is important. An ex-Marine named Elston Hubbard opens the card impressively, knocking out his opponent in one minute, twenty seconds and foreshadowing a key event later in the novel. He is mature, strong, and confident. Even Bud is impressed.

The ritual for Alfred is the same as it is for Donatelli's professional fighters. He even receives an impressive white robe with his name on the back in red letters. The lessons Alfred is learning are as important as any match: If he listens to Donatelli, he does well; if he does not, he is on the canvas.

Henry's role expands in this chapter. He is responsible for Alfred's welfare throughout the hours leading up to the fight and is an assistant trainer in Alfred's corner. He also serves an important function within the novel, because it is Henry who tells Alfred that police raided the clubroom and found marijuana and heroin. James was there during the raid, but he escaped arrest, as did everyone except Sonny and Justin.

Lipsyte's verbal imagery is impressive again, specifically his use of verbals. An ice ball in the gut symbolizes Alfred's pre-fight fear. Just as the bout is to begin, the ice ball explodes, "spraying his entire body with freezing, paralyzing streams of water, weighing down his arms, deadening his legs, squeezing his heart." No wonder Rivera's first punch nails Alfred. Still, all the training pays off. Alfred bounces off the ropes jabbing. His legs are "steel springs"; his arms are "whips." Alfred has been superbly prepared, if he follows Donatelli's instructions.

Theme

Bill Witherspoon and his wife, Betty, serve as examples of life beyond the ring. Even on this day of Alfred's crucial first fight, they talk with him about education. The living room of their modest apartment houses more books that Alfred has ever seen in a home. Henry points out that the couple uses the books to settle arguments, like whether a black man was the first to reach the North Pole. Alfred laughingly compares this to an argument at James' house when his friend's parents threw whiskey bottles at each other in a dispute over cigarettes; a bottle hit James in the head, and it took nine stitches to close the wound.

Bill and Betty transcend racial stereotypes in other ways as well. They live in a racially mixed neighborhood. Alfred notices this and asks Spoon if he has white friends. Spoon says he has a few, joking that he decided to allow whites to move into his neighborhood when he saw that white boys' blood is the same color as his.

Lipsyte avoids being preachy or didactic, but this is a novel about a young man's education and maturation. There are some lessons along the way.

Glossary

Washington Heights a residential district in northern Manhattan, New York City; here, the area of New York in which Bill and Betty Witherspoon live.

polio short for "poliomyelitis," an acute infectious disease, especially of children, caused by a viral inflammation of the gray matter of the spinal cord; it is accompanied by paralysis of various muscle groups that sometimes atrophy, often with resulting permanent deformities; here, the disease that crippled Henry Johnson.

terry-cloth a pile fabric, usually woven of cotton, used to make towels and robes; here, the fabric in the robe Alfred receives before his fight.

Chapter 16

Summary

November brings Alfred's second amateur fight, this one against a very fast and skillful boxer named Griffin. Donatelli wants Alfred to move in against Griffin and use combinations as he did when sparring against the speedy Angel. Alfred tries but runs into the red blur of Griffin's gloves. The first two rounds are all Griffin's, as he stings Alfred with what seems like hundreds of pitter-pat blows. Alfred needs a knockout.

In the third round, Griffin tires and begins to miss. Alfred hits him with a combination, the last punch a magnificent hook that leaves Griffin twitching and then lying dead-still on the canvas. Alfred wins the fight but feels alone and sick. He wonders if he has killed Griffin. He has not, but the image haunts him through the next day.

Commentary

In this chapter, Lipsyte provides the first indication that Alfred may not have the killer instinct necessary for a career as a professional boxer. Alfred is developing well and wins a fight that he could easily have lost, but he is more concerned that he might injure his opponent than he is with winning.

Lipsyte's imagery is descriptive and apt. Griffin is no puncher, but the repeated blows feel like the stings of a hundred bees and leave Alfred swollen and dazed. Griffin's gloves are "a red blur tapping away at Alfred's face, easy and steady as rain on a roof, pitter-pat, pitter-pat." Alfred stands a chance only after Griffin wears himself out hitting Alfred's face. The months of training come into play as Alfred is able to call on reserves of fitness and skill, and a beauty of a hook, to deck the opponent. Instead of being elated, however, Alfred feels sick.

Theme

A brief appearance by Harold and Lynn, the young black nationalists, foreshadows an eventual development in the novel. They want Alfred to become involved in a recreation program for the youth of the community. They feel that the kids would respect a boxer. As Lipsyte reveals in the next chapter, the idea is to develop black leadership that the children can relate to and respect, because, too often, whites (to whom the kids have difficulty relating) have run such programs.

Chapter 17

Summary

The family gathers at the home of Uncle Wilson and Aunt Dorothy for Thanksgiving. Despite Wilson's usual display of pompous authority, Alfred thinks it is the best Thanksgiving ever. He is surprised that he gets along so well with his cousin Jeff, the college boy. Jeff expresses an interest in boxing, and Alfred is curious about his cousin's plans after college. Initially intending to work in Africa with the Peace Corps, Jeff is having second thoughts. He wonders if he might not do more good by staying home and working with black communities in the inner-city. Alfred surprises Aunt Pearl by expressing an interest in finishing high school. He and Jeff discuss the idea of black recreation centers.

When Alfred returns home, the appearance of James, who looks like a "shuddering old man" hiding behind a garbage can near the front entrance to the building, disturbs Alfred. James wants help, in the form of money. When Alfred offers food and shelter, James insists that he needs money for just one more fix. With regret, Alfred gives him six dollars, and James immediately takes off.

Commentary

Character Insight

This chapter foreshadows the ending of the novel in two ways. First, we discover that Alfred has mixed feelings about boxing. He enjoys the workouts and the camaraderie at Donatelli's Gym, but the violence of the sport bothers him.

As Alfred and his cousin Jeff become friends, he and Jeff find a common ground in their belief that they can contribute to a growing independence of the black community. The new Alfred pleasantly surprises Jeff. He recalls an Alfred who "seemed to just drift along." This recalls how Alfred noticed, in Chapter 12, the "hungry-eyed" faces on street corners in Harlem, hopelessly waiting for something to happen. Alfred is no longer likely to join tem. Now he wonders if he might be able to finish his high school education and provide leadership in a recreation center. Alfred quotes Spoon repeatedly; the schoolteacher obviously has inspired him.

James' return to Alfred's life contrasts with the bright hopes of the Thanksgiving holiday. James is now in the depths of his addiction. It is appropriate that he hovers behind a garbage can. James' eyes, once bright and full of life, are sunken. He shivers inside a torn overcoat. All he can think of is another fix. As Alfred continues to find himself, James is lost.

Chapter 18

Summary

Alfred has two matches scheduled in December. The first is against a fighter named Barnes who is not as quick as Griffin or as strong as Rivera but is a rough customer who fights dirty. Donatelli's approach is to have Alfred stick and move, punishing Barnes while staying away from him. Alfred defends himself but offers very little offense. The fight is a draw. Back at the gym after the fight, Donatelli tells Alfred that it is time to quit boxing; but Alfred insists that he must fight one more time.

Commentary

Lipsyte uses this fight to show that Alfred does not belong in the ring. Alfred is reluctant to hit Barnes because he keeps thinking of Griffin twitching on the canvas after Alfred knocked him out in his previous fight. When the crowd boos the boring performance, Alfred dismisses the fans as bloodthirsty louts.

Mr. Donatelli cares most about Alfred as a person. He tells him frankly that he does not have the killer instinct necessary to succeed in the ring; further, Donatelli says he is not sure he would want Alfred to have it. The scene reminds us of the caring way that Donatelli told Spoon to stop fighting and pursue other goals. Alfred argues that some fighters don't have a killer instinct. Donatelli agrees but adds that those are exceptionally talented boxers. He candidly adds that Alfred is not that good.

The mentor reminds his protégé of the first night that he climbed the stairs to the gym. The staircase has become one of the most consistent metaphors in the novel. It represents Alfred's ascension toward maturity and his continuing effort. That first night, it was a monstrous, terrifying barrier. On his next visit, they were "friendly old steps" that he bounced up two at a time. When he wanted to quit, they were "crummy steps"; he had to stop twice to catch his breath. This trip, he walks with Donatelli for the first time, slowly climbing the "sagging stairs."

Alfred insists that he must fight the one match left on his schedule to finish what he has begun. Donatelli warns him that Alfred's record probably will cause him to be matched against a fighter who is much better than his previous opponents. He could get hurt. Alfred reminds Donatelli of what the manager once said about being a *contender*. He can't quit until he has really tried. Alfred understands that he can be a contender in life as well as in the ring, but he must first finish what he has started and prove to himself that he is a contender.

Chapter 19

Summary

Alfred prepares for his last fight, at Parkway Gardens in Brooklyn, as he did the others, but he is noticeably more nervous. The fight will be the climax of Alfred's climb, just as, structurally, it is the climax of the novel. All other activity has led to this crescendo.

As they wait at Spoon's apartment, Henry tries to calm Alfred and reflects on his own budding career as a trainer. Alfred is especially important to the neophyte assistant manager because he was the first fighter entrusted to Henry by Mr. Donatelli. Henry reveals that it was he who bought the white terry-cloth robe for Alfred prior to the first fight. He feels that he has found his role in managing; he doesn't limp as much now that he has more important things to think about. After Alfred retires from the ring, Donatelli will allow Henry to train some of the newcomers.

Spoon arrives and tells of an altercation at school with a boy named Herbert Davis who pulled a knife on him. He spent the afternoon counseling Davis, suggesting that he go to the gym to try boxing. Foreshadowing the novel's ending, Spoon tells Alfred that he has spoken with a doctor at a narcotics clinic about James; but Alfred says that he has not been able to find his old friend in the neighborhood.

In the dressing room before the bout, an official informs Donatelli that the only available opponent for Alfred is Elston Hubbard, the older, bigger ex-Marine who was so impressive opening the card the night of Alfred's first fight. Donatelli wants to cancel the match, concerned that Alfred will be hurt. Alfred reminds the manager that Donatelli once told him that the only sure way to judge a fighter is to see him when he is hurt. Alfred feels that he *must* fight Hubbard.

Hubbard is overwhelming. Alfred is on the canvas within seconds of the sound of the opening bell. He is down again before the first round ends. His performance improves some in the second round; he manages to jab and move, to fight back, and he is only decked once. During the break between the second and third rounds, the referee asks Donatelli if he wants the fight to continue. Henry asserts himself and insists that Alfred must have his chance. Donatelli says, "Let him fight."

Round three is a war. Alfred takes tremendous punishment but stays on his feet, standing toe-to-toe with Hubbard and fighting as well and as hard as he possibly can. Neither man hears the final bell; they have to be pulled apart.

In a unanimous decision, the judges correctly declare Elston Hubbard the winner of Alfred's last boxing match, but Donatelli knows that Alfred has won the most important fight. Back in the locker room, he is smiling when he says, "Now you know, Alfred. Now you know, too."

Commentary

As a sportswriter, Lipsyte recognizes the importance of ritual to sport, and he uses it as an effective structural device. As usual, Henry accompanies Alfred to Spoon's apartment after lunch. This allows them to have time alone, during which Henry reveals more of his character. Whereas Alfred doesn't really like fighting, as Mr. Donatelli observes near the end of Chapter 18, Henry *does* love managing. The reader gets the idea that Alfred will go on to successful pursuits in other professions; but years later, Henry will still be managing fighters. Henry may be the next Donatelli.

The fight itself is a classic, all the more significant because we know from the start that Alfred cannot win. Hubbard embodies all of the strengths, and more, of Alfred's sparring partners and former opponents. He is stronger, faster, rougher, and more skillful than all of them. Finally, we know from Chapter 14 that he is a welterweight, at least seven pounds heavier than Alfred.

Hubbard is a quick starter; true to his form, he explodes into Alfred at the opening bell and scores a knockdown. As the fight progresses, Lipsyte's imagery is specific and telling. Hubbard's left is "like a meat hook." His head crashes into Alfred's mouth. He hurls the lighter man against the ropes. His gloves are hammers. His shoes slash at Alfred's ankles. Hubbard's shoulders rough up Alfred's chin. His head is like a huge bullet, grinding into Alfred's eyes. Alfred has no business staying in this fight. In a magnificent simile, embodying the life of Alfred the street kid, Lipsyte describes the sound that Alfred numbly hears as he is knocked down a second time; it is a "distant plop, like a stone splashing into the pool at the bottom of a sewer hole."

Still, Alfred fights back. He manages to throw some combinations. In the second round, he is better, sticking and moving. Unfortunately, Hubbard catches him in a corner, slamming Alfred against the post. The ex-Marine's fists are sledgehammers. Alfred is down for the third time. Somehow he is up again, telling the referee that he is fine. He survives the second round, and Henry succeeds in convincing Donatelli to allow a third.

Alfred is seriously hurt. His vision is blurred. The crowd is insane. He faces a bigger, better, meaner fighter. He cannot win. And he doesn't care. He stands toe-to-toe with Hubbard. He will not back off. He is "gonna stand here all day and all night, . . . gonna climb, man, gonna keep climbing, you can't knock me out, nobody ever gonna knock me out, you wanna stop me you better kill me." Alfred goes the distance. Lipsyte foreshadows that Alfred will always go the distance; it just won't be in a boxing ring.

Glossary

Brooklyn a borough of New York City, on western Long Island.

Chapter 20

Summary

When Alfred returns home after his last match, Aunt Pearl is visibly upset. Alfred quickly explains that he is so late because everyone went to eat at a restaurant where Jelly now works. However, Aunt Pearl is not concerned about Alfred's tardiness or even the injuries to his face. James is in trouble. He broke through Epsteins' front window earlier that night, cutting himself but escaping as the police arrived. He is hurt and in hiding. Alfred knows where, and he takes off running to find him.

James is in the cave in the park when Alfred arrives. He is bleeding badly from a cut on his arm but is more concerned about scoring another fix. Alfred wants to take him to the hospital, warning James that he could lose his arm if not his life if he does not get medical attention soon. Alfred reminds James of their long friendship and encourages him about the future, but James has little hope. He says the police will arrest him. James fears incarceration for violating probation rules. As for the future, he is sure that "Whitey" won't allow him to succeed. Alfred quickly tries to convince James to adopt a different attitude, but his old friend has not learned the lessons of life that now bolster Alfred and help him to overcome adversity. Finally, Alfred simply acts as though he is leaving. Facing isolation, James gives in. With James leaning heavily on Alfred, the two exit the cave and start for the hospital.

Commentary

The book ends as it began, with Alfred in search of James. Their friendship is one of the key themes in the novel, and it adds to the structure. Up to the first attempted burglary of Epsteins' grocery, when Alfred refused to participate, the lives of the two ran parallel. After that break, Alfred ascends while James declines. Now, Alfred literally and figuratively hopes to lift James, keep him alive, and help him find his way. Alfred recalls that James was there for him the night his mother died and that the two often shared their dreams, some of which were unrealistic, some possible. When James asks why he is doing this,

Alfred responds confidently, "Because I know I can, James. And you're my partner."

Even in the brief scene in the cave, we see that the lessons of Donatelli's code have been woven deeply into the fabric of Alfred's character. He wants to pass them on to his friend. When James denies that he is an addict, Alfred immediately confronts him with words that recall the scene near the end of Chapter 17 when James crouches behind a garbage pail: "Look at you, like a garbage rat. You hooked all right."

Alfred relies on some of Donatelli's statements, as well as the mentor's philosophy. When Alfred tries to encourage James about the future, the addict sardonically interrupts that he probably will be just a "grocery boy." Alfred has learned to respect that exact opportunity and echoes Donatelli in his response: "For start. Nothing's promised you, man . . ." Nor does Alfred tolerate James' excuse that "Whitey" will never allow him to succeed. Alfred the fighter says, "Dare him to stop you."

Character Insight

Alfred has come a long way. When they were younger, it was James who seemed the stronger. He stood by his friend when Alfred's father deserted his family and when his mother died. When Alfred dropped out of school, it was James who tried to dissuade him. But James soon dropped out, too, and serious character flaws were hidden beneath the surface. Now, Alfred is clearly the leader. As Donatelli put it in Chapter 3, he is the man who is climbing, the man who knows he may never reach the top but is willing to "sweat and bleed to get up as high as his legs and his brains and his heart will take him." Alfred has become a *contender*.

CHARACTER ANALYSES

Alfred Brooks

Alfred Brooks is a black seventeen-year-old high school dropout who lives with his Aunt Pearl and her three daughters in Harlem. His father deserted the family when Alfred was ten years old; his mother died when he was thirteen. Alfred's story parallels the major theme of the novel, which is stated most poignantly by the fight manager, Mr. Donatelli, near the end of Chapter 3, in his speech that begins, "You have to start by wanting to be a contender." A contender is, first and foremost, a man, an adult. For the true contender, the journey is more important than the arrival. Donatelli tells Alfred that a contender is willing to pay the price. He will "sweat and bleed" to get as high as his talent, courage, and character will take him. Of course, Donatelli is speaking about life as well as boxing.

Although he has dropped out of high school, Alfred has accepted responsibility in life. Unlike James and the gang members, he has a job. Aunt Pearl praises him for that and says that she will not treat him like a little boy. But this is a "coming of age" story. At the beginning of the novel, Alfred only *dreams* of a life as an adult. Part of that dream is to transcend the repressive atmosphere of the mean streets of Harlem. The novel tells the story of *how* he achieves his dream.

Henry, a physically disabled acquaintance who aspires to become a fight manager, urges Alfred to visit Donatelli's Gym, which is famous for having trained several boxing champions. Alfred's climb up the staircase to the gym is symbolic; he is beginning his climb toward maturity. At the gym, he meets Donatelli, a wise mentor. The manager tells Alfred that nothing is promised. He should be sure that he wants to make a real effort; quitting is worse than never starting at all. Something in Alfred wants to succeed, so he begins training.

Becoming a contender is more difficult and tedious than Alfred imagined. Discouraged and frustrated, he attends a Friday night party at the neighborhood street gang's hangout, a basement clubroom. Allowing the gang's leader, Major, to influence him, Alfred spends much of the night drinking and smoking marijuana. Sunday morning, he accompanies the gang to Coney Island in a stolen car and spends most of the day running, alone, from the police. He decides to quit training.

While cleaning out his locker at the gym two nights later, Alfred experiences a kind of epiphany, a moment of clarity or self-awareness. Speaking with Mr. Donatelli, he begins to wonder if he ever could have made it as a contender. He realizes that he must try.

After more training, Alfred is allowed to spar and finally to have his first amateur fight. His opponent is another lightweight named Rivera, a powerful but relatively immobile puncher. Alfred does well, as long as he follows Donatelli's advice to "stick and run." When he disregards Donatelli's advice, he ends up on his back. Alfred wins the fight, but he still has a long way to go to accomplish his goal of being a contender.

Griffin, Alfred's second opponent, is quick but not much of a puncher. Following Donatelli's instructions, Alfred attacks, pressuring the weaker man. Nevertheless, Griffin is more skillful and wins until Alfred catches him with a tremendous hook in the last round. Griffin is knocked out; he lies twitching on the canvas. Alfred fears that he has killed him.

Alfred's next fight is a draw because he is reluctant to attack the opponent, afraid that he may seriously injure him, too. Donatelli asks him to retire, but Alfred recalls the manager's words about becoming a contender. He must finish what he has started. Although he loses his final bout, Alfred fights with all he has. He goes the distance.

At the end of the novel, Alfred wants to finish high school and work with youngsters in the community, passing on some of Donatelli's wisdom. He is able to use his newly found maturity in rescuing his best friend, James.

James

As the novel opens, James Mosely is Alfred's lifetime best friend. However, James has already started on a path opposite Alfred's. In the novel's first chapter, James joins Major and the gang in an attempted burglary of Epsteins' grocery. Although Alfred inadvertently tells the gang that cash may be in the register overnight, he flatly refuses to go along. James does, however, and is arrested during the break-in.

Most significant is James' embodiment of another theme of the novel: hope versus despair. While Alfred hopes for a better life, James has already given up. He despairs. When we see him at the Friday night clubroom party near the end of Chapter 11, he is in the throes of drug abuse. His teeth are yellow with neglect. His face is thin and his eyes sunken. He speaks as though he is stoned. When James returns to Alfred on Thanksgiving night, his only interest is finding enough money for his next fix. At the end of the novel, when Alfred has "climbed" to become a true contender in life, not just in the boxing ring, James is at his lowest. He has broken through the front window of Epsteins' store in a dangerously clumsy attempt at another burglary. His arm is seriously cut.

As soon as Alfred hears that James is on the run, he knows where his friend is hiding. Alfred finds James in their secret cave at the park where they shared so many boyhood dreams. Even then, near the point of death or imprisonment, James prefers to wallow in racial despair, blaming "Whitey" for his problems. To Alfred, this is a poor excuse, because Alfred has learned to combine his hope with some tough love and realistic effort. We have the feeling that Alfred will triumph in life. Whether he will be able to pull James up with him is up to James.

Mr. Donatelli

Vito Donatelli has seen it all. He has worked with world champions like Sugar Ray Robinson and with punks like Red, the boastful egocentric fighter who foolishly takes a swing at Bud Martin near the end of Chapter 6. Donatelli has shaped a philosophy from his lifetime of watching and learning.

First, nothing is promised to anyone at Donatelli's Gym—or, we might infer, in life. Everyone is treated the same; each boxer is given only what he earns. Donatelli respects hard work, perseverance, and character more than raw talent. He values the process more than the result, the journey more than the arrival. He is the boss in his own gym, but he believes in giving people a second chance. Most importantly, Donatelli urges Alfred to be a contender, in life as well as in boxing. In both arenas, Donatelli tells Alfred he should let the championships come if they will, but he should not dwell on them. Set the goal for each day's work, not for the final result. Donatelli knows that, for most fighters, life beyond the ring will be more important than anything they do inside the ring.

Spoon

Bill "Spoon" Witherspoon is the novel's best example of the Donatelli code put to practice. Spoon had been a promising light-heavyweight boxer, ranked seventh in his division. He was still winning fights when Mr. Donatelli said, "Billy, I think it's time," meaning Donatelli thought it was time for Spoon to quit boxing. It was time for Spoon to retire because, even though he was winning, Spoon was being beaten too hard in the ring. Donatelli told Spoon to use the money from his wins, which the wise old manager had forced him to save, to return to college full time. Spoon became a teacher, married another teacher named Betty, and lives in a racially mixed neighborhood in Washington Heights, an area of Manhattan. Within the context of the novel, Spoon serves as exemplar to Alfred, helping to prepare him for his bouts but primarily encouraging him to finish high school and do something more with his life.

Major

Major is the antagonist of the novel. He represents the cynical, repressive, manipulative side of Harlem that Alfred initially fights to escape and ultimately learns to overcome. Leader of the gang that hangs out at the basement clubroom, Major would like to bring everyone down to his level or, preferably, just below him. He first tries to intimidate Alfred. When Alfred finally stands up to him, Major tries to befriend the novel's protagonist. He uses Alfred's best friend, James, as bait in an attempt to lure Alfred into a life of drugs, alcohol, and despair—a life in which the choices are few and Major is boss. Major is dangerous because he tempts Alfred to give up the way James has. Alfred succeeds when he can stand up to Major and find a life more rewarding than hanging out on street corners or in the clubroom.

Aunt Pearl

Aunt Pearl Conway provides a home and a moral context for Alfred. At least initially, she may be the difference between Alfred's hope and James' despair. She works hard for the white Elversen family, setting an example of effort that Alfred follows. A good Christian woman who tries her best, she still needs help in guiding Alfred into manhood. Pearl's role in the novel is enhanced when we learn that she, too, had dreams of a career, in singing, when she was Alfred's age, but unlike Alfred, she didn't see whether she could be a contender. That experience informs her and helps her to accept Alfred's choices.

Aunt Dorothy and Uncle Wilson

Pearl's sister and her family live in the suburban community of Jamaica in the borough of Queens. They represent the flight of the black middle class from Harlem after World War II. Whenever given half a chance, Uncle Wilson articulates the theory that a black man's best interest is served by escaping the slums. Although the argument has merit, Wilson's own college-educated son, Jeff, is beginning to wonder if he might not do more good by working within communities like Harlem. All of this influences Alfred who thinks only of escape early in the novel but grows to an understanding of service within the community by the novel's closing chapters.

Lou Epstein

Lou Epstein is one of three brothers who own the store where Alfred works as a grocery clerk. Although the brothers have given Alfred a job, they come to distrust him after the attempted burglary by Major and the gang. The Epsteins know that Alfred and James were friends, and James is the one perpetrator who is caught. Lou, however, takes a special interest in Alfred, partly because Lou was once a respected fighter himself, known as "Lightning Lou Epp." Lou ultimately believes in Alfred and offers him the opportunity to work the store's cash register.

Lou is another person who encourages life beyond the ring for Alfred. Lou and his brothers are also significant because they are Jewish shop-owners in predominantly black Harlem. As such, they are part of a difficult social dilemma and easy targets for racial slurs by Major in Chapter 1.

CRITICAL ESSAYS

Setting as Symbol

Essential to a full appreciation of *The Contender* is an understanding of Lipsyte's use of setting. The world in which Alfred lives is Harlem, a predominantly black community on the northern end of Manhattan in New York City. Within the context of the novel, Lipsyte introduces various aspects of Harlem as well as other locations around the city. Lipsyte uses these settings as major symbols. Each setting represents a different side of life and affects Alfred in its own way.

When Alfred first appears in the novel, he is on the front steps of the building that houses his Aunt Pearl's apartment. Before him are the mean streets of Harlem. The atmosphere is repressive. The sun, often a literary symbol of hope or promise, melts into the despair of a "dirty gray Harlem sky." The air is "sour," rancid, and foul. Young men without direction gather on street corners, drifting, waiting for something to happen. Cars crunch through garbage and broken glass. Packs of children, "ragged and skinny," have empty beer cans for toys. The sights and sounds echo the sense of the backdrop that Lipsyte paints. This is the world that dominates Alfred's life. His struggle will be to overcome the repression. Initially, Alfred thinks he can do this only by escaping Harlem.

Aunt Pearl's apartment offers some security, but it can't compare to Aunt Dorothy and Uncle Wilson's suburban home in Queens. Dorothy's home represents the flight of the black middle class away from Harlem and into the suburbs after World War II. The streets are clean and grassy, lined with attractive houses. The food is abundant and good. Wilson discourages concern for those left behind in the inner-city. When Alfred returns to Harlem, the streets seem dirtier, the apartment smaller. The plaster cracks over the kitchen sink. A roach scurries across the cabinet. Addicts scuffle in the hall. Alfred sleeps in a fold-up bed. At this point, Alfred yearns for escape.

Knowing no better way, Alfred and his best friend, James, have spent much of their childhood trying to escape their lives through fantasy. The movie theater symbolizes an important means of escape for the boys. While watching a movie, they can enter a world of action and adventure. Interestingly, they often side with the hero's adversaries. Identifying with the underdogs, they cheer for the Indians to defeat the cowboys and for the monsters to prevail. On the streets, Alfred also sees men whom he admires, adults with suave manners and sophisticated ways, like the characters he sees in the movies. When a pretty girl his age sits beside him on the subway in Chapter 4, he longs for some kind of crisis so the he can come to her rescue, introducing himself as the leading man might in a movie: "I'm Alfred Brooks, may I be of service?"

Television serves as another means of escape for Alfred. On television, Alfred sees more of the fantasy world beyond Harlem: a speeding stagecoach, shooting Indians, "Uncle Harry" on a children's show greeting the "Kiddie Klubbers." The people on television are almost always white, and they live in a world foreign to Alfred. In Chapter 2, he watches a white family whose mother is pretty and slim and whose husband is tall and handsome. Their kitchen is shiny and as big as Aunt Pearl's entire apartment. The dog, Gus, can romp across a huge lawn under trees. Little Billy, their son, secretly builds a robot in the garage. At seventeen, Alfred is skeptical about the accuracy of the depiction, but he wonders if some people really do live that way.

Much of Alfred and James' dreaming is shared at a secret cave that James discovered in the park as a young boy while rock hunting. He had a book about rocks and wanted to save the best ones to show at school. When James took the rocks home, however, his drunken father dumped them all down the air shaft in their apartment. At that moment, it is as though James' dreams were dumped down the air shaft as well. One of James' dreams was to be an engineer and build great things. But James allows himself to believe Major and Hollis when they tell him that "the white man" would never allow him to build anything but garbage heaps.

The cave is a safe place for James and Alfred, a symbolic haven from the mean streets and bullies like Major who steal whatever small change the boys have. Near the end of the novel, when James is seriously injured and running from the police, Alfred knows that he can find his old friend hiding in the cave. As boys, they spun their dreams in solitude there. Some of their fantasies may have been unrealistic, but at least Alfred and James had hope. James doesn't have much hope left as the novel opens; his hopes and dreams have been dashed by people like his father and Major and the gang.

In sharp contrast to the secret cave is the clubroom where the street gang hangs out. The clubroom is Major's domain and symbolizes the negative energy of Harlem. The mean streets make themselves at home in the basement hovel; the gang members strut right in, flop on the sagging couch, and light up a joint. Major literally flexes his muscles in front of the cracked mirror, watching a distorted reflection that delights him. He enjoys flexing muscles, bullying people, pushing and manipulating them. Major is not stupid; he is a talented mimic, and he usually knows which buttons to push to get others to do his bidding. In order to get Alfred to attend the Friday night party, for example, Major tempts him with a promise that James will be there. When Alfred arrives, Major already has a girl and other temptations (such as alcohol and drugs) waiting for Alfred. Alfred sees the party as another means of escape. The problem is that this escape is destructive if not deadly. Alcohol and drugs are not harmless daydreams. They leave Alfred physically crashed and morally spent as he heads for Coney Island in the stolen white Cadillac convertible with the gang the next day.

Coney Island symbolizes Alfred's lowest moment. It is more like a descent into hell than an amusement park. Alfred is lost, injured, hot, and hung over. He vomits on himself and is shunned by strangers. But even at this lowest point, some hopeful things happen. Alfred refuses to blame his plight on Major or anyone else. Alfred alone accepts responsibility for attending the party and going to Coney Island with the gang. When he returns to Harlem, Alfred notices the hungry eyes on the lost faces of young men standing on street corners, waiting for something to happen. Although he decides to quit boxing, a spark of hope remains, as evidenced by Alfred's meeting with Mr. Donatelli when Alfred returns to the gym, ostensibly to clean out his locker, two nights later. Donatelli ignores him until Alfred initiates the conversation. Alfred then realizes that he really wants to try to be a contender.

Donatelli's Gym is the antithesis of the mean streets. At the gym, Alfred finds a world with a practical code of ethics. Everyone has an equal chance. Alfred will receive only the benefits that he earns. Nothing is promised to him except a fair chance. To get to the gym, Alfred has to climb. The gym is on the third floor of a building, and those three flights of stairs represent a psychological as well as a physical ascent for Alfred. The staircase is not a pretty place. It smells of stale wine, antiseptic, sweat, urine, and liniment. Alfred's legs shake; a ball of ice is in his gut. Thousands of steps seem to loom before him. They are so steep that he falls to all fours sometimes, just to keep going. His teeth grind, and his throat is dry; but Alfred makes it to the top. At the gym, he learns the most important lessons of his life and prepares for the test of the fight ring.

The union hall on Long Island where Alfred has his first amateur match is about as far away from Madison Square Garden as he can get. The Garden is the ultimate in the sport of boxing. It is where the best fighters go to perform before thousands of knowledgeable fans and sometimes, through television, the eyes of the world. The union hall is just a shabby building with a sleepy old man at the door and a locker room filled with cigar smoke. Places like this are where boxers start. They represent a chance, but little more. However, the boxing ring itself is the same in all of the arenas, whether at the union hall or Madison Square Garden. The ring is where Alfred must be tested, on character even more than on ability. The lessons at the gym were Alfred's homework. His final exam is the match with Hubbard, which takes place at Parkway Gardens in Brooklyn.

The final fight is where Alfred has the opportunity to prove to himself that he truly is a contender. Although he is outmatched, Alfred gives everything he has and goes the distance against a bigger, stronger, and better fighter. Although he loses a unanimous decision, Alfred is everything that Mr. Donatelli said a contender must be. He is a man who realizes that he probably will never be a boxing champion but is willing to give all he has to go as far as his abilities and character will take him. He does not quit. He knows that quitting would be worse than never starting in the first place.

When Alfred returns to the cave to help James in the final chapter, he carries with him the lessons that he has learned at the gym and in the ring. Most importantly, he knows that these are lessons for life, not just for boxing. Ultimately, he will deal with Harlem as he dealt with Hubbard in his final match: by facing it, going toe-to-toe, refusing to run, and going the distance.

Major Themes

The Contender is a coming-of-age novel, and its major themes are universal. They do not apply just to Alfred or to boxing or to Harlem. The themes of *The Contender* inform all of us about life, which is Mr. Donatelli's point from the moment that he first talks with Alfred. Donatelli's code applies to all of life, not just to boxing. In addition to being universal, the novel's themes are intertwined, making it difficult to separate them. Even when one theme seems separate and distinct, it reflects the others.

The first theme that we encounter in the novel is that the true importance of friendship is to be there for your friend but not to sink with him if he chooses to sink. Alfred is devoted to his best friend,

James, and he is willing to do almost anything for him. Alfred is concerned when James does not show up to go to the movies with him, but he knows his friend well enough to guess exactly where he is. At the clubroom, Alfred, the protagonist of the novel, must encounter his primary antagonist, Major, leader of the street gang. Major pretends to be a friend of James, just as he later pretends to be Alfred's friend; but Alfred knows that Major only wants to drag James down and control him. Although Alfred is devoted to James, he knows that friendship must have limits. James sticks with the gang even though they taunt and insult Alfred. Alfred wants to be with James but draws the line when the gang leaves to break into Epsteins' grocery. When James chooses to go down that road, Alfred does not follow. He would rather be alone than with "friends" like that. Nevertheless, Alfred is there for James in his friend's most desperate moment at the end of the novel. Alfred is a true friend because he wants James to be all that he can be.

Mr. Donatelli introduces most of the novel's major themes when he first meets Alfred in the gym in Chapter 3. Before Alfred even begins training, he wants the young man to understand that quitting before you really try is worse than never starting at all. Alfred has already dropped out of high school, but, despite his early history of quitting, Donatelli wants him to understand that he expects an honest effort if Alfred starts training. Donatelli is realistic enough to know that Alfred may quit, but he wants Alfred to realize that it is wrong to do so. Donatelli has a code of ethics. Right and wrong are serious matters to him. Near the end of the novel, Alfred is true to this theme when he insists on going ahead with his final bout, even when he realizes that it is against an older, bigger, and better fighter. Alfred refuses to quit during the fight and goes the distance, which is what Donatelli now knows that Alfred will do in life.

For Donatelli, the journey is more important than the destination. This theme affects everything that the wise old manager does. It explains why the daily grind of training is more important to him than a championship fight and why he treats every fight the same. Donatelli knows that what we do in our daily lives reflects what kinds of people we are. The process is more important than the result, because our characters determine our daily effort. The end result, the destination, will take care of itself.

From the beginning, Donatelli impresses Alfred with the fact that nothing is promised you. There are no guarantees in boxing *or* in life. Alfred learns this theme so well that it is the first thing that he impresses on James when he helps him in the cave at the close of the novel: "For start. Nothing's promised you, man, but you ain't gonna know nothing till you try." Alfred uses this motto to confront the harsh realities of his own life. Racism alone can not stop him because he doesn't expect any guarantees in the first place. He *expects* the struggle to be difficult.

Throughout the novel, Alfred learns that he is responsible for the choices that he makes. Alfred seems to grasp this concept of accountability in Chapter 12, when he realizes that he can't blame Major for what happened at the party or at Coney Island. Alfred has made his own choices and must live with them. By the same token, Alfred *chooses* to continue training, to go ahead with his final bout, and to finish the fight even though he is clearly losing. Ultimately, Alfred will choose whether to flee Harlem or try to work with young people there who face the same problems he faced.

The biggest difference between Alfred and James is that Alfred, for all his doubt, genuinely believes that hope will triumph over despair. It is why he keeps trying, and it is why James quits. Alfred's fights symbolize this. Every time he gets knocked down, he gets up. He sees other boxers who quit when they are hurt, but Alfred just fights harder. Even against Hubbard, when he knows he can't win, he keeps getting up. Through his actions, Alfred says to Hubbard what he is thinking: "[Y]ou can't knock me out, nobody ever gonna knock me out, you wanna stop me you better kill me."

The novel takes its title from the most important theme, which Donatelli articulates best: "You have to start by wanting to be a contender." All of the other themes evolve from this one. By focusing on his character and progress on a daily basis, rather than just dreaming of being a champion, Alfred becomes a contender in life and can be a true friend to James. Finally, he has a place within the community and, like Donatelli, something to offer others.

Style Enhances Substance

Lipsyte's writing style enhances the substance of his story in *The Contender*. He reveals Alfred's life primarily through his own eyes. Lipsyte's occasional similes and metaphors are particularly apt; his dialogue and imagery are powerfully effective.

For the most part, Lipsyte uses a third-person narrative, limited to insight into Alfred's mind. We see the story through Alfred's eyes. The narrative is linear, which means that it proceeds within a certain time-frame from beginning to middle to end. We usually know what month it is and often which day of the week. The setting or context is New York City, usually Harlem, from June to December of a year in the mid-1960s. Although Lipsyte presents no actual flashbacks, Alfred often recalls events from the past in such detail that the reader might feel that he has witnessed them. An example of the power of this kind of memory is the discovery of the cave with James, which took place ten years before the action of the novel.

The author makes selective use of *similes*, comparisons using the words "like" or "as." When Aunt Pearl takes her little girls to church on Sunday at the beginning of Chapter 4, they sail past the rough-talking nationalist speakers "like starched white tugboats escorting a blue cotton ocean liner." We get a sense of the size of Aunt Pearl, compared to the size of the girls, as well as a sense of Aunt Pearl's devotion to direction. She is not the least distracted from her Sunday morning voyage. Although that simile is as wholesome as Aunt Pearl, many of Lipsyte's similes are as rough as the boxing ring. When Alfred awakes on the day of his first match, he notices that the plaster over the kitchen sink has broken loose, leaving "a powdery-white hole as big as a fist." This simile helps to set the scene for Alfred's day, in which this child of poverty will try to break through to a better life, using his own fists. One of the most effective of Lipsyte's similes describes Hubbard's second knockdown of Alfred in the final fight. Alfred hears a "thud against his ear and then the distant plop, like a stone splashing into the pool at the bottom of a sewer." The simile echoes the violence of the ring as well as the harsh reality of the mean streets that Alfred knows so well.

Sometimes Lipsyte chooses *metaphor*, a figure of speech in which the author speaks of something as if it actually were something else. At the opening of Chapter 12, for example, Alfred is passed out on his kitchen floor, somehow having returned home from the wild party at the clubroom. Lipsyte writes that Alfred hears a rattlesnake buzzing. But in fact, the noise Alfred hears is the ringing telephone. Alfred's subconscious transfer of *telephone* to *rattlesnake* reveals his aversion to the constant harping of the trainers. He feels pressured by time. He thinks Henry is screaming at him and Jelly Belly is sitting on his head. The rattlesnake is a deadly threat, and Alfred thinks that life is attacking him. At other times, Lipsyte writes of punches that *are* tons of concrete or iron pipes, rather than saying that the punches *felt* like them. Under attack, Alfred sees the punches that way. The dominating metaphor of the novel, however, extends beyond any one scene. The fight game, Mr. Donatelli would tell us, is life. It is not "like" life or "as real as" life. It *is* life. And that is the basis of all of Donatelli's *aphorisms* (brief statements of principle). Alfred finally understands. As he says to Mr. Donatelli near the end of Chapter 18, "Remember what you said that night . . . about being a . . . a contender? . . . You weren't just talking about boxing."

The language may be cleaned up a little, but the dialogue in the novel is usually realistic. In the very first chapter, we get a clear look at Major's personality through the way he speaks. He is a manipulative bully who loves to mock. When Alfred says that he has given his pay to his aunt, Major mimics him derisively: "Gave it to my aunt . . . You such a good sweet boy. Old Uncle Alfred." Later, Major, who apparently never works, compares Alfred's job at the grocery to slavery. Major mocks the stereotypically "shufflin'" personality that he accuses Alfred of displaying to his Jewish bosses: "You be scratching your head and saying, 'Yassuh, Mistuh Lou, lemme brush them hairs offen your coat . . . I be pleased iffen you 'low me to wash your car.'" In contrast, Mr. Donatelli speaks in a straightforward, candid manner, as in his first meeting with Alfred: "It's hard work, you'll want to quit at least once every day. If you quit before you really try, that's worse than never starting at all. And nothing's promised you, nothing's ever promised you."

Lipsyte's imagery is especially powerful. Imagery is not always visual. It can appeal to any of the senses: sight, sound, taste, smell, or touch. In *The Contender*, the author moves quickly from one specific image to another. The opening page of the novel, for example, asks the reader to see, hear, and even smell the Harlem neighborhood where Alfred lives. The very air is acrid and repressive. The sky at twilight is "dirty gray." Lipsyte leaves his readers a little stunned that even young men fortunate enough to have automobiles and "Friday night girls" must cruise through garbage and broken glass. In only a page of text, Lipsyte evokes a setting that informs the reader precisely.

Contrast the novel's opening page with the first paragraph of Chapter 5 when Alfred experiences his first training run. Here, the air is "cool and sweet." The sky is "blood-red," filled with vigor and dawn life. Alfred can't keep the smile off his face. If he had the breath, he'd sing. He is so in tune with nature that the birds not only chatter, they share "all the bird gossip." For more than a moment, Alfred is in a new world that foreshadows the vitality that his future may hold. Throughout the novel, the imagery is especially effective. Some examples are Alfred's various ascents of the stairs to the gym, his experiences in the gym, his visit to Madison Square Garden, his attendance at the clubroom party, his trip to Coney Island, and Lipsyte's descriptions of the fights.

An author is not necessarily aware of every stylistic device as he is creating a novel. As readers, we must understand that at least *some* of an author's style is instinctive; it feels right or sounds right. But the total effect is that the style enhances our connection to the story. And Lipsyte's style is no exception.

CliffsNotes Review

Use this CliffsNotes Review to test your understanding of the original text, and reinforce what you've learned in this book. After you work through the review and essay questions, identify the quote section, and the fun and useful practice projects, you're well on your way to understanding a comprehensive and meaningful interpretation of *The Contender*.

Q&A

1. The setting of the novel is an area of New York City known as _____.

2. After James quits school, he begins to hang out with a gang led by _____.

3. Alfred's first run in the park is interrupted, and ruined, by _____.

4. Alfred hits the heavy bag to learn power but the peanut bag to improve his _____.

5. Bill Witherspoon is a positive role model whose profession now is _____.

6. Lou Epstein was once a fighter known as _____.

7. Alfred's regular job is at _____.

8. Alfred's last fight is won by _____.

9. Near the end of the novel, Alfred knows that James will be hiding at _____.

10. The major theme of the novel is that it is more important to be a _____ than a champion.

Answers: (1) Harlem (2) Major (3) two policemen (4) speed and/or timing (5) teaching (6) Lightning Lou Epp (7) Epsteins' grocery (8) Elston Hubbard (9) the cave in Central Park (10) contender

Identify the Quote

1. I see you now, boy, old and stooped. . . . Old and stooped. You be scratching your head and saying, "Yassah, Mistuh Lou, lemme brush them hairs offen your coat; yassuh, Mistuh Jake, I be pleased iffen you 'low me to wash your car."

2. Everybody wants to be a champion. That's not enough. You have to start by wanting to be a contender, the man coming up, the man who knows there's a good chance he'll never get to the top, the man who's willing to sweat and bleed to get up as high as his legs and his brains and his heart will take him. That must sound corny to you.

3. Yes, sir, Alfred, world is changing. Me, I never was past the county line until the war came. Now your cousin Jeff's been all over the country. Talkin' about joining the Peace Corps after college, going to Africa. Got a letter from him the other day, says he's going to be ready when the opportunities come.

4. Remember what you said that night . . . about being a . . . a contender? . . . You weren't just talking about boxing. . . . And what you said about quitting before you really tried. . . . You got to let me finish.

5. Dare him to stop you. Dare anybody if you and me partners again. . . . Even if they send you away, won't be forever. I'll be around. Gonna get you clean, man, and gonna keep you clean. . . . Because I know I can. . . . And you're my partner.

Answers: (1) Early in the novel, Major uses stereotypes to mock Alfred's attempt to make something of himself working at Epstein's grocery. (2) During his first visit with Alfred, Donatelli introduces him (and the reader) to the central theme of the novel. (3) Although he can be trite and annoying, Uncle Wilson wants to guide Alfred toward a better life, as he does in this passage. (4) Prior to his last fight, Alfred tells Donatelli that he *must* finish what he has started. (5) At the end of the novel, Alfred tries his best to help James overcome his addiction to drugs and find a better life.

Essay Questions

1. Discuss the friendship between Alfred and James. Consider its limitations as well as its history and future possibilities.

2. Analyze Spoon's character and his influence on Alfred. Refer to specifics of his life and to conversations between the two characters.

3. As a sportswriter for the *New York Times*, you are assigned to interview Mr. Donatelli. Write a news story about the interview, quoting your questions and Donatelli's responses.

4. Discuss the role of racism in the novel. Try to include all aspects of the problem.

5. Define one of the major themes of the novel and discuss how Alfred's character relates to it.

6. Choose one specific setting in the novel and show in detail how Lipsyte uses imagery to develop mood.

7. What do you think James will do after the novel ends? Discuss his future.

8. If you could choose one character in the novel to be your friend, other than Alfred, who would it be? Why?

9. Why is Aunt Dorothy's family important in the story? As part of your answer, discuss each family member's significance.

10. In your own life, what would it mean to be a "contender"?

Practice Projects

1. Create a Web site to introduce *The Contender* to other readers. Design pages to intrigue and inform your audience, and invite other readers to post their thoughts and responses to their reading of the novel.

2. Choose a scene from the novel and dramatize it for other classes. The production will require putting the scene in play form (freely adapting according to inspiration), assigning roles, directing, and staging the production. Follow the performance with a discussion of the novel's themes.

CliffsNotes Resource Center

The learning doesn't need to stop here. CliffsNotes Resource Center shows you the best of the best—links to the best information in print and online about the author and/or related works. And don't think that this is all we've prepared for you; we've put all kinds of pertinent information at www.cliffsnotes.com. Look for all the terrific resources at your favorite bookstore or local library and on the Internet. When you're online, make your first stop www.cliffsnotes.com, where you'll find more incredibly useful information about *The Contender*.

Books

This CliffsNotes book provides a meaningful interpretation of *The Contender* published by IDG Books Worldwide, Inc. If you are looking for information about the author and/or related works, check out these other publications:

Critical Works about Lipsyte

Authors and Artists for Young Adults, Volume 7, edited by Laurie Collier. Detroit: Gale Group, 1991:139.

Contemporary Authors, New Revision Series, Volume 57, edited by Jeff Chapman and John D. Jorgenson. Detroit: Gale Research, 1997:323.

Presenting Robert Lipsyte, by Michael Cart. New York: Twayne, 1995.

Literature for Today's Young Adults, 2nd Edition, by Kenneth L. Donelson and Alleen Pace Nilson. Glenview, Illinois: Scott, Foresman, 1985.

Lipsyte's Published Works of Fiction

The Brave. New York: HarperCollins, 1991.

The Chemo Kid. New York: HarperCollins, 1992.

The Chief. New York: HarperCollins, 1993.

The Contender. New York: Harper & Row, 1967.

"Future's File." *Within Reach: Ten Stories*, edited by Donald R. Gallo. New York: HarperCollins, 1993.

Jock and Jill: A Novel. New York: Harper & Row, 1982.

One Fat Summer. New York: Harper & Row, 1977.

Summer Rules. New York: Harper & Row, 1981.

The Summerboy: A Novel. New York: Harper & Row, 1982.

Lipsyte's Published Works of Nonfiction

Arnold Schwarzenegger: Hercules in America. New York: HarperCollins, 1993.

Assignment: Sports. New York: Harper & Row, 1970. Revised and expanded edition, New York: Harper & Row, 1984.

Free to Be Muhammad Ali. New York: Harper & Row, 1978.

Idols of the Game: A Sporting History of the American Century. Atlanta: Turner Publishing, 1995.

In the Country of Illness: Comfort and Advice for the Journey. New York: Alfred Knopf, 1998.

Jim Thorpe: 20th-Century Jock. New York: HarperCollins, 1993.

Liberty Two. New York: Simon and Schuster, 1974.

The Masculine Mystique. New York: New American Library, 1966.

Nigger: An Autobiography, by Dick Gregory with Robert Lipsyte. New York: Dutton, 1964.

Something Going, by Robert Lipsyte and Steve Cady. New York: Dutton, 1973.

Sports and Society, edited by Robert Lipsyte and Gene Brown. New York: Arno Press, 1980.

SportsWorld: An American Dreamland. New York: Quadrangle/New York Times Book Company, 1975.

It's easy to find books published by IDG Books Worldwide, Inc. You'll find them in your favorite bookstores (on the Internet and at a store near you). We also have three Web sites that you can use to read about all the books we publish:

* www.cliffsnotes.com

* www.dummies.com

* www.idgbooks.com

Internet

Check out these Web resources for more information about Robert Lipsyte and *The Contender*:

Africana.com, www.africana.com — an excellent resource for African American history and culture.

Alfred A. Knopf Web Site, www.randomhouse.com/knopf/aak/qna/lipsyte.html — an interview with Robert Lipsyte.

The Cyber Boxing Zone, www.cyberboxingzone.com — a boxing encyclopedia, with lively audio and visual.

Hungry Mind Review: An Independent Book Review, www.book-wire.com/hmr/review/recom.html — book reviews for teens.

University of Southern Mississippi Young Adult Novel Reviews, www-dept.usm.edu/%7econnect/reviews.html — reviews of young adult novels by college students.

Wautauga High School Web Site, www.ced.appstate.edu/whs/contende.htm — student reviews of *The Contender*.

Next time you're on the Internet, don't forget to drop by www.cliffsnotes.com. We created an online Resource Center that you can use today, tomorrow, and beyond.

Films

The following films may be of use when studying Robert Lipsyte and *The Contender*:

Idols of the Game, Bobkat Productions and TBS Originals, 1995. Hosted by Dabney Coleman. A documentary film about sports idols written by Robert Lipsyte.

Shining Star (also known as That's the Way of the World). Dir. Sig Shore. Perf. Harvey Keitel and Bert Parks. United Artists-Marvin, 1975. A feature film written by Robert Lipsyte.

Check your local library or video store for these films.

Magazines and Journals

Check out these magazine and journal articles for more information on Robert Lipsyte, *The Contender*, and boxing:

Plimpton, George. "Sports: How Dirty a Game?" *Harper's Magazine*, September 1985: 45.

Robinson, George. "The 24-Year Comeback." *Publishers Weekly*, 26 July 1991: 11.

Scales, Pat. "*The Contender* and *The Brave* by Robert Lipsyte." *Book Links*, November 1992: 38.

Simmons, John S. "Lipsyte's *Contender*: Another Look at the Junior Novel." *Elementary English*, January 1972: 116.

Spencer, Pam. "Winners in their Own Right." *School Library Journal*, July 1990: 23.

Send Us Your Favorite Tips

In your quest for knowledge, have you ever experienced that sublime moment when you figure out a trick that saves time or trouble? Perhaps you realized you were taking ten steps to accomplish something that could have taken two. Or you found a little-known workaround that achieved great results. If you've discovered a useful tip that helped you study more effectively and you'd like to share it, the CliffsNotes staff would love to hear from you. Go to our Web site at www.cliffsnotes.com and click the Talk to Us button. If we select your tip, we may publish it as part of CliffsNotes Daily, our exciting, free e-mail newsletter. To find out more or to subscribe to a newsletter, go to www.cliffsnotes.com on the Web.

INDEX

CliffsNotes

LITERATURE NOTES

Check Out the All-New CliffsNotes Guides